FIELD & STREAM'S

Guide to the Outdoors

FIELD & STREAM'S

GUIDE TO HUNTING

T. EDWARD NICKENS
AND THE EDITORS OF FIELD & STREAM

Gareth Stevens
PUBLISHING

FIELD & STREAM'S Guide to the Outdoors

FIELD & STREAM'S
GUIDE TO
HUNTING

T. EDWARD NICKENS
AND THE EDITORS OF *FIELD & STREAM*

Gareth Stevens
PUBLISHING

CONTENTS

"There is a passion for hunting something, deeply implanted in the human breast."

—Charles Dickens

Born in a Tree Stand

We were bird-dogging the tundra like wolves, stalking through blueberries, bearberries, and cranberries with bows in hand. Deep in Alaska's Brooks Range foothills, somewhere north of the Yukon River, my buddy and I were road-weary and grimy with sweat from a freakish heat wave. And we were hungry.

Suddenly, two ptarmigan silhouettes popped up in the tundra, unmoving. I drew a judo-pointed arrow and settled the 25-yard pin on the near bird. A stiff breeze sent tufts of cotton grass tumbling in the air, so I shifted the sight three inches to the left and released. The bird crumpled, and four more appeared out of nowhere.

With the thwack of each shot, ptarmigan popped up like prairie dogs. We drew, aimed...and suddenly the target took off running. I took three steps and tripped, two steps and drew. Within minutes, seven birds were down and scattered across a half acre of tundra, and arrows lay everywhere. Across a shallow gully, my buddy Scott Wood held up a pair of ptarmigan by their feathered feet. "Finally," he hollered, "the red gods smile!"

We knelt down to study each ptarmigan, mottled brown feathers going to winter white, cradled in tundra grasses just beginning to turn with autumn's reds and golds. We gutted them on the spot, stuffed them into our vests, and headed back to camp.

There is something elemental about hunting, something deep-seated and hard-wired that links us to the land. There's a direct line that can be drawn from finger to trigger to stomach to soul.

Even when wild game isn't required to fuel our day-to-day needs, the pursuit itself is a sinew that ties us to a favorite clearing in the woods, a particular bend in a river.

All hunters have felt this. Ojibwa and Shawnee. Seminole and Creek. The Georgia swamper and the Midwestern farm boy and the weekend warriors who flee the city for weekends in the woods.

The great beauty about hunting is that it takes so many shapes and so many forms that you can spend all of your life trying to do everything just once. Ducks or deer, squirrels or moose—rifle, shotgun, muzzleloader, bow. Is there any other pastime that opens the door to more of the world? Is there anything more American than a man or woman in the woods with a gun, free to roam, his or her purpose to take a life in order to sustain life?

I don't think so.

But let's not overdo all of the spiritual mumbo-jumbo. We might hunt to put food on the table and stay in tune with earth, wind, and sky, but we also choose to go after deer and ducks and rabbits because it's just plain fun.

Following bird dogs through skin-shredding briars? Fun.

Walking in your waders to pick up a duck that fell across the creek channel? Fun.

Packing an elk out of the dark timber, two miles in and two miles out and three trips to get it all? We're the only ones who understand this, but, yes, even that's fun. At least, it will start to seem that way a few months later.

For many of us, hunting defines who we are in ways that defy explanation. We may not remember the first time we caught a football or even our first kiss, but we remember the first time we pulled a trigger. We remember those first hunts, when we were glowing iron on the anvil ready to be shaped by stories and places and people and sleepless mornings. We know when we became hunters.

The first time I went deer hunting, I was 13 years old. A friend of my dad had been taking me squirrel hunting for a couple of years, and after he listened to me whine about deer hunting for months on end, off we went. I remember following his footsteps

through dark woods, and then he stopped and pointed his flashlight toward a tree. When he walked off, I was as scared to death as I'd ever been. I'd hunted with Keith many times, but never away from his side. Never alone.

That old climbing stand was a handmade job, and back then few folks thought to make a separate climbing seat so you could sit and stand your way up an oak. Instead, you bear-hugged the tree with your arms, hooked your boots into the metal frame of the climber, pressed your face into the bark and hung on with all your strength. Pulled your knees to your chest. Repeat. By the time you reached a decent height, your clothes were soaked with sweat, your hair was matted with sap, and you barely had enough arm strength left to lift a bow or gun.

After about 15 minutes of this torture, I figured I was so high I might soon run out of tree, so I stopped, my chest heaving, and settled in to hunt. As the sun rose and the woods lightened, I looked around and realized that the only way I was going to kill a deer that morning was if it ran through the woods so fast that when it hit its head on the climber it would break its neck. I was only a few feet off the ground.

But I remember clinging to that tree, a piece of rope knotted around my scrawny belly, forearms swollen and bloody, and telling myself that it didn't matter if I killed a deer or not. Because I was on my own, in the woods with a gun. No longer was I just a kid tagging along. From that day to this, I was a hunter. —*T. Edward Nickens*

1 IDENTIFY DRAKE MALLARDS FLYING

Here are four simple steps that let you tell a greenhead from a girl duck before you pull the trigger.

SIZE MATTERS At first light, before you can see the green of a mallard's head, shoot the larger duck. Nine times out of ten, the bigger duck in a pair is a drake.

BE PATIENT Hold back and let the birds work the decoys so that you can get a good look.

KEEP YOUR EARS TO THE SKY
Listen before you launch a load of No. 2s. Mallard hens quack. Mallard drakes call with a low, reedy yeep-yeep call that will identify them instantly.

KEEP YOUR EYES ON THE BELLY
Look for the "halter top," the hard line between the drake's brown neck and white belly. —T.E.N.

If you've hunted long enough, you know how humiliating it feels to send an arrow over a deer's back or put a bullet in the dirt. The good news: You may never feel that way again. Here's how to keep your shirttail intact.

STABILIZER Adding a stabilizer is the easiest way to steady your bow and improve your shooting. Don't skimp on weight.

THE MIND It's the most important aspect of shooting. You must deliberately focus on keeping your form perfect, shot after shot. If you think about aiming, accuracy will suffer.

RELEASE ARM Keep steady backward pressure with this arm until the arrow goes off. Think of it as pulling your bow apart.

RELEASE MOTION Don't start and stop. Commit to a good follow-through, and the release will occur naturally.

BOW ARM A weak or tight bow arm causes most misses. You need to apply steady forward pressure here, right into the target.

STANCE Keep your feet lined up perpendicular to the target, which is the easiest way to maintain the same stance for each shot.

Keep your wrist "low," as in fully flexed backward, with the bow grip contacting your hand at the heel of your palm. A bone there gives you solid contact. Your fingers should be relaxed. If you're holding the bow correctly, at full draw your knuckles will line up at a 45-degree angle, halfway between 7 and 8 on an imaginary clock.

BOW

Few skills rely so heavily on the connection between body and mind as does shooting a bow. From the soles of your feet to the position of your head, it all has to come together. —B.H.

SWING HAND In order to maintain control of the muzzle, make sure your hand is forward enough on the fore-end to effect a smooth swing.

EYES Don't ever take your eyes off the bird. Looking from bird to muzzle to bird will cause you to miss.

THE SWING You need to pick up the target, see it clearly, and decide where you're going to break it. When it's in the right spot, pull the trigger, and follow through.

Start with the toe of the stock at waist level or a little above. The muzzle should be pointed where you expect to intercept the bird.

MOUNT Don't slap the butt into your shoulder; doing so will jolt the muzzle out of position and you'll need more time to pick up the target. Your shotgun mount must be fast and consistent. Good shots don't waste any motion.

The gun should describe a slight arc outward as you bring it up to keep it from catching on your clothing. Your head stays erect as the stock meets your cheek.

FOOTWORK Your feet should be pointed at an angle to the target so you don't have to fight to get the muzzle around.

When the butt is in your shoulder, your head should have to come down very slightly to be in shooting position. Your right elbow should be parallel to the ground, left elbow a bit lower.

SHOTGUN

As athletic an endeavor as drilling a 50-yard field goal or sinking a 30-foot putt, shooting a shotgun requires focus and coordination. —D.E.P.

THE ZONE To find your natural point of aim, put the crosshairs on the target, close your eyes, relax, breathe, and open your eyes again. If you're no longer on target, you have to adjust your position.

RETICLE Focus on the intersection of the crosshairs, not the target, when aiming.

HANDS Twist both hands downward slightly as if wringing a towel. This allows you to control the rifle as it recoils.

SHOULDER Pull the buttstock securely into your shoulder.

ELBOWS Keep your elbows angled down at about 45 degrees.

KNEELING POSITION Take one step toward the target with the support-side leg (here, the left). Pivot on the ball of the strong-side foot and kneel as shown. The flat part of the supporting elbow rests on the supporting knee, with the rifle held directly above.

STANCE Stand nearly square to the target, angled slightly toward your strong side (here, the right side). Keep knees slightly flexed and lean into the rifle with the weight on the balls of your feet.

RIFLE

Nothing comes closer to the heart of American hunting than this: Hit the target. Precisely where you aim. Every time. —P.B.

SQUATTING POSITION From your natural point of aim, squat straight down, with feet flat on the ground. Turn toes outward if necessary. Points of elbows are forward of the knees, with flat part of the supporting elbow resting on the knee directly below the rifle.

3 DISAPPEAR WITH A CORK

Toss a cork and a lighter into your hunting pack, and you'll never be without a way to hide one of the biggest warning signs to game—your face. First, give the end of the cork a pre-burn treatment. Hold the lighter flame an inch below the tip until it smolders and flames. Rub out the black smudge on a piece of paper and then repeat. Once you get a good charcoal tip, it takes just a few seconds with a lighter to rejuvenate the cork before you apply it to your face. Cork camouflage washes off much more easily than commercial paints.

To carry your cork, store it in a zippered plastic sandwich bag. And be sure you're using real cork, not synthetic. —T.E.N.

4 GRILL STUFFED BACKSTRAPS

The best venison backstrap you'll ever eat is also one of the most impressive cuts to serve—and very easy to master. Here's what you need.

INGREDIENTS

One piece of venison backstrap
Italian dressing
Cream cheese
Fruit chutney
Bacon
Sun-dried tomatoes (optional)
Onions, carmelized (optional)

Marinate backstrap in Italian dressing for 12–24 hours. Butterfly by slicing horizontally through the meat to within one-half inch of the far side.

Open the butterfly cut lengthwise, like a sub sandwich roll. Add quarter-inch slices of cream cheese and then cover each with the fruit chutney. (Cranberry and mango work well. For a more subdued version, replace the chutney with sun-dried tomatoes or carmelized onions.)

Close up backstrap and wrap with bacon.

Truss the backstrap with kitchen string. Begin by looping the string around one end and then tie it around that end with a double overhand knot. Next, stretch 2 inches of string along the backstrap. Hold it in place with your thumb, wrap the string around the backstrap, pass the string behind your thumb, and repeat to wrap the entire backstrap. At the end, pass the string on the other side of the meat, threading it under the wraps. Tie off to the first wrap, and you're done.

Grill until medium rare. Snip off the string, slice, and serve. —T.E.N.

5 PLANT A MICRO FOOD PLOT

Farm and beaver ponds are perfect for seeding with Japanese millet strips, which ducks relish. It's easy and cheap and very effective. Here's how.

SCHEDULE IT Summer heat will often draw pond levels down, or you can lower the pool with flashboard risers. Millet matures in about 60 days. Plan with opening day in mind. Stagger the planting over a few weeks; plant deeper areas first and then move up the bank. That will keep the feed coming for a month.

RAKE IT If you're seeding mud, simply broadcast on the surface. For drier soils, use a steel rake or an ATV rake to score.

SEED IT Plant Japanese millet at the rate of 20 pounds per acre. You want to plant the seeds about an inch and a half apart. Plant it too densely and you'll stunt the growth of the new stems.

FEED IT Use one bag of 13-13-13 fertilizer per bag of seed and fertilize when the millet is 12 to 18 inches tall. —T.E.N.

6 ADJUST A SADDLE FOR AN ALL-DAY HUNT

After planning a horseback hunting trip for months, many desk jockeys finally arrive in big-game country barely able to walk, just due to the ride in. The secret to success is paying attention to the length of your saddle's stirrup leathers, which connect the stirrups to the saddletree. This is the primary factor that determines whether your trail will take you to lifetime memories or salty tears. Here's how to adjust your stirrups to fit your legs.

ON THE GROUND Get in the ballpark by running your hand under the seat to where the stirrup straps touch the saddletree. Adjust the length of the leathers so that the stirrup bottoms reach to your armpit.

IN THE SADDLE Fine-tune the fit by letting your legs hang down naturally from the saddle. Adjust the stirrup so the bottom of the tread is slightly below your anklebone. Now stand in the saddle. You should have a fist-size clearance between the saddle and your butt. If you're a greenhorn, it's wise to err on the shorter side.

IN YOUR MIND Adjust your expectations—riding over long distances hurts. There's an old saying: "If your knees are sore, your stirrups are too short. If your butt is sore, your stirrups are too long. If both your knees and your butt hurt like fire, then everything is just right." —T.E.N.

7 PLOT A SHOT WITH YOUR COMPUTER

Use Google Earth's mind-blowing database of searchable satellite imagery to figure out shot distances long before you pull the trigger. First, call up Google Earth and pull up your hunting location. Go to the top toolbar and click on "Show Ruler." Next, click on the down arrow beside the blue window that says "Miles," and change the unit of measurement to "Yards." Now your cursor will function as crosshairs. Click on the starting point for measurement and move the cursor to the ending point. Distance will show up in the window. —T.E.N.

FIELD & STREAM-APPROVED KNOT

8 RIG A PRUSIK-KNOT SAFETY ROPE

When it comes to danger, climbing into your tree stand could be said to rank right up there next to hunting rhinos with a pellet rifle. Learn to climb with a safety rope tied with a Prusik knot clipped to your harness, and you'll dramatically increase your chances of one day being a crotchety old fart. Tie off a rope to the bottom of the tree and then to the trunk above the level of your head when you're standing up in your stand. Tie a Prusik knot around this safety rope, and slide it up and down as you go. —T.E.N.

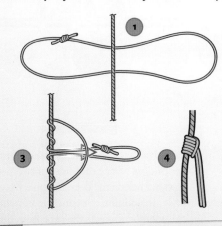

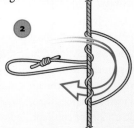

After the last pass, push the end with the knot under the other end of the loop. Tighten the knot evenly, taking care not to allow the winds to overlap.

9 REMOVE A BACKSTRAP WITH PRECISION

Many hunters ruin the best cut of venison. To avoid doing this, begin by hanging the deer from its hind legs and removing the shoulders.

STEP 1 Insert the knife beside the spine right in the middle of the deer. Keep the blade tight against the vertebrae and cut down to the neck. Turn the knife around and extend the cut to the hindquarters until the knife hits the pinbone of the hip. Repeat on the other side of the spine.

STEP 2 Insert your knife out in the curve of the ribs, 4 inches from where you think the edge of the backstrap lies. Carefully work the knife along the curve of the ribs and the bottom of the vertebrae to meet your long cuts. Be sure to bring all the rib meat out with the backstrap.

STEP 3 Make the final cut across the backstrap at the pinbone, connecting the two long incisions. —T.E.N.

10 HAUL YOUR DEER ANY DISTANCE

One tagged deer, no cart, no ATV, no dragging harness, and miles to go before you sleep. So what's the most efficient way to haul that animal out of the woods? Here are two methods to try. Both get your deer's head, neck, and shoulders off the ground, which results in less friction and easier dragging.

ONE-PERSON DOE DRAG Cut a sturdy stick of about ¾-inch diameter to an 18-inch length. Whittle a point on one end. Stab an inch-long slit through the animal's muzzle with your knife, just behind the black part of the nose and across the top of the nose bone. Work the knife blade under the cartilage and out the other side of the muzzle. Insert the stick into this slit. Grab the dragging stick with both hands behind your back.

TWO-PERSON BUCK PULL Pull the front legs forward and tie each tightly to the base of an antler. Then lash a stout 4-foot-long stick to the antlers at a crotch in the tines, leaving enough length protruding from either side for two people to stand beside the deer and pull, oxen-style. In addition to easing the burden, this method protects the cape from dirt and abrasion. —T.E.N.

11 TEACH A BIRD DOG TO POINT

Getting a bird dog pup to start pointing feathers has as much to do with training as instinct.

GET THE PUP IN FEATHERS For the first year, it's all about getting the dog into birds. You want your pup to find so many birds that he figures out there's no way he can actually catch them.

GET TO THE DOG Once the dog points, get there fast. Your pooch needs to see the bird shot in front of him. That's the positive reinforcement.

GET THE POINT ACROSS Never shoot at a bird that he hasn't pointed. Teach your dog that the only way he's ever going to get a bird in his mouth is to point it so you can shoot it.
—T.E.N.

12 FACE A DUCK BLIND IN THE RIGHT DIRECTION

Sometimes there's no choice, but on a cloudless day, an east-facing setup will force you to shoot into the glaring sun during the critical first half hour of legal light.

A front-lit blind also stands out from its surroundings more than a blind set in the dark shadows. Some hunters argue that drawing a bead on birds silhouetted against the light in the eastern sky is easier, but you'll disagree after five minutes of frying your retinas once the sun has topped the horizon. —T.E.N.

13 KILL A WILD PIG WITH A KNIFE

For centuries, Hawaiian natives dispatched wild pigs with little more than gumption and a 6-inch blade. As wild pig populations explode across the country, hunting them with dogs and a knife is growing in popularity. Here's the drill—if you dare.

STEP 1 Approach the pig from the rear, while it's focused on the dogs. Move slowly and avoid getting between your quarry and anything that would prevent you from backing away.

STEP 2 Grab the pig's hind legs just above the hooves. Lift the animal up like a wheelbarrow. The pig will fight for a few seconds and then stop. Flip him over on his side. Have a buddy secure the dogs away from the pig.

STEP 3 Let go with your knife hand and get a knee on the pig's shoulder. Unsheathe your knife. Sink it low and behind the shoulder, so it enters the heart, and then remove the blade immediately. Keep your weight on the pig until the deal is done. Pull this off correctly, and it takes mere seconds. —T.E.N.

14 WALK LIKE A SHADOW

Spring woods are noisy. A carpet of dead leaves and a winter's worth of ice-felled branches litter the forest floor. Learning how to walk silently will put you in a better position to call in the gobbler of a lifetime—and help you walk up to a hat-rack buck next deer season.

WALK LIKE A CAT Begin your step by lifting your foot straight up, toes pointing down to avoid snagging. Place the outside of your foot down first. Press the ball of your foot into the ground consciously, rolling from the outside in. Bring down your heel, then slowly shift weight to that foot. Be prepared to lift and shift whenever you feel any obstacle that might snap or crackle under your weight.

MAP YOUR STEPS To avoid having to watch your feet, make a mental map of the upcoming ground cover for the next 8 to 10 paces. Especially note where you might need to sidestep branches or high-step over fallen logs.

GO SLOW When looking for game, take three to four slow steps and stop. How slow? Three steps should take you at least 20 seconds.

HIDE YOUR NOISE Mask the noise of footfalls by moving whenever other sounds can muffle your own. Wind in the trees, moving water, and even airplane noise can all hide the sound of a human on the hunt. —T.E.N.

15 KNOW YOUR NUTS

Nothing draws game like mast crops, be they oak, beech, or hickory. The trick is knowing which crop is which, and what critters can't pass them by. —T.E.N.

WHITE OAK

In a good year, a mature white oak can produce upwards of 2,000 acorns. White oaks typically produce "bumper" crops every three to four years.

BEST FOR Deer, squirrels, turkeys, grouse, bears

CHESTNUT OAK

These sweet acorns are among the largest mast fruits in the woods and sprout soon after they fall. Deer can't eat enough of them.

BEST FOR Deer, squirrels, turkeys, bears

RED OAK

Red oaks are higher in tannin than white oaks, so deer target acorns of the latter first. But in years with a wet, cold spring or a late spring frost, white oak acorn production often plummets. A stand in red oaks pays off.

BEST FOR Deer, squirrels, turkeys, grouse

CALIFORNIA BLACK OAK

This western oak doesn't mind rocky slopes, thin soils, and dry climates. It's critical for muleys, and fawn survival rates are tied to its mast production. Look for pure groves loaded with acorns.

BEST FOR Mule deer, bears, quail

AMERICAN BEECH

Once the oily beechnuts are released from their prickly husks, smaller animals prize them. Wild turkeys will cover a lot of ground to find a good beech ridge; the extinct passenger pigeon once flocked to such spots.

BEST FOR Deer, squirrels, turkeys

SHAGBARK HICKORY

It's the sweetest hickory nut in the woods. Squirrels love them, and their gnawing sounds are a giveaway to knowing hunters. Wild turkeys swallow the nuts unshelled and let their gizzards do the hard work.

BEST FOR Squirrels, turkeys

16 HOST A SUMMERTIME BACKYARD ARCHERY TOURNAMENT

Between the last bite of watermelon and the campfire, you've got a lot of afternoon to fill, so break out the bows for a few rounds of Archer's Horse. In this version, you'll spell A-P-P-L-E-P-I-E (or U-S-A for a quick game). First, set up a few 3-D targets at various distances and angles. On each, designate a small high-risk marker by sticking a high-visibility adhesive dot (or leftover hamburger bun) on, for example, the neck of the deer or the throat of a bear. Next, establish a line that shooters can't cross when it's their turn. When you've arranged the course and shooting order, here's how to play:

CALL IT Shoot from anywhere along the line and however you'd like—standing, kneeling, singing the national anthem. And you must call your shot: "Vitals, whitetail target."

SHOOT IT If you hit your target, the second shooter has to match the shot. If he makes the same shot, it falls to the third

shooter to do the same, and so on until either someone misses or everyone makes the shot, at which point the first shooter takes a new shot.

MOVE IT If someone misses the shot, he is assigned a letter and moves to the last slot in the shooting order. The shooter who's next in line becomes the new leader and decides the next shot.

RISK IT To make things interesting, a shooter may call a high-risk shot during his turn. If he misses, he automatically gets a letter. But if he hits the target, it's worth two letters to the first player to miss the shot.

WIN IT When a shooter is assigned his final letter, he's not written off yet. He gets one more attempt at the shot—but this time he must hit the high-risk marker. If he nails it, he loses a letter. If he misses, he has to fetch hot dogs for the remaining shooters. —T.E.N.

17 WET-AGE A DEER

Aging venison allows naturally occurring enzymes to break down the structure of collagen and muscle fibers. That helps tenderize the meat and gives it distinctive, complex flavors. But early-season deer hunters—and deer hunters all season long in the sunny South—have a tough time hanging deer when it's warm out.

To age venison in balmy weather, try wet-aging. Cool the carcass with ice for at least 12 hours; butchering a deer before rigor mortis sets in can turn even tender cuts chewy. While butchering, remove as much silverskin and connective tissue as possible; keep whole muscles as intact as you can. Drain off blood, pat the cuts dry with a paper towel, and then package the butchered meat in vacuum-sealed bags. Store in a refrigerator for five to eight days. After aging, freeze the cuts as they are or finish butchering them into portion sizes.

Wet-aging won't give your venison the complex, concentrated flavors that would accrue during a week in a frosty barn. But even in the fridge, enzymatic action will go to work on silverskin and tendons, turning a warm-weather September buck into a meal worth bragging about. —T.E.N.

18 TRY REAL BRUNSWICK STEW

You could argue forever over the birthplace of the famous Brunswick stew. Perhaps it's Brunswick County, North Carolina. Brunswick County, Virginia? Brunswick, Georgia? The state legislatures of Virginia and Georgia have even passed proclamations boasting bragging rights. But no one fights over its original primary ingredient. Squirrel it was, and squirrel it still is. Earmark a bitter-cold Saturday for stirring up a simmering pot of Brunswick stew. It's best cooked over an open fire. This recipe makes about 10 servings.

INGREDIENTS

- 4 large onions, diced
- 5 tbsp. bacon fat
- 6 to 8 squirrels, parboiled and deboned
- 6 cups water
- One 28-oz. can diced tomatoes
- 1 cup apple cider
- 2 tsp. Worcestershire sauce
- 2 pounds fresh or two 10-oz. packages frozen lima beans
- 2 cups fresh or frozen corn kernels
- Salt and pepper to taste
- 2 tsp. red pepper flakes
- 1 cup seasoned bread crumbs
- 4 tbsp. melted butter

In a Dutch oven, fry the onions in bacon fat and then remove them. Without draining the fat, add the squirrel meat and cook until it's browned. Add the water, tomatoes, cider, and Worcestershire sauce. Simmer partially covered for 30 minutes. Add the lima beans and corn and simmer for 30 minutes. Add salt, pepper, and red pepper to taste. Sprinkle the bread crumbs, drizzle the butter over the top, and then stir. Cook uncovered for 15 to 20 minutes more. It's ready when a sturdy wooden stirring paddle will stand straight up in the pot. —T.E.N

19 PICK THE RIGHT GUN

The type of mechanism used to load, fire, and eject rifle cartridges and shotgun shells is called the "action." Single-shot firearms must be reloaded after each shot. Repeating firearms fire each time the trigger is pulled, with additional cartridges or shells held in a magazine or tube under the gun barrel. Choosing which action you want in a firearm is critical, and the right decision balances speed, safety, accuracy, gun-handling characteristics, and aesthetics. —T.E.N.

SHOTGUNS

BREAK-ACTION SINGLE BARREL With a hinge at the receiver, break-action firearms open like a door to expose the breech for loading. Because single-barrel guns of this type can be made short and light, they are often a young shooter's first firearm.

SIDE-BY-SIDE This break-action shotgun features a pair of barrels mounted beside each other. Quick pointing and elegant, short and well balanced, this is the traditionalist's go-to gun, especially for hunters of upland birds such as quail. Many are made with double triggers—one to a barrel—for an instant choice of which choke to use.

OVER/UNDER A more modern variant of the break-action double-barreled shotgun, the over/under is a favorite of American shooters. It offers a quick follow-up shot, a choice of chokes for varying shooting conditions, and a single sighting plane down the top barrel.

PUMP A repeating shotgun, this action is worked by the shooter cycling the fore-end back to remove the spent shell and cock the firing pin and then forward to chamber the fresh shell and close the action. Fast, smooth, and dependable, pump shotguns are a favorite of waterfowl hunters due to the relative lack of moving parts and ability to work even when wet and muddy.

SEMIAUTOMATIC Also known as "autoloaders," these actions automatically cycle new shells into the chamber each time the shotgun fires. Gas-operated semiautomatic shotguns use some of the gas created when the shell is fired to work the action. Recoil-operated actions use the force of recoil to move the bolt and chamber a new shell. Autoloaders are quick to fire numerous shots and have less recoil than other actions but are generally heavier and bulkier than other actions.

SINGLE SHOT Single-shot rifles must be reloaded after every shot. Break-action single-shot rifles are opened at the breech for reloading. Other examples include the "falling block" single-shot action, in which the breech is opened by moving a lever on the underside of the gun. Single-shot rifles are very safe to operate, very accurate, and very strong.

BOLT ACTION By far the most-popular action among hunters, the bolt-action rifle is opened and closed manually by lifting and pulling a protruding handle that looks similar to a door bolt. Closing the bolt chambers a fresh round, which is lifted from a magazine located underneath the action. Strong and dependable, the bolt action is very accurate.

PUMP ·Pump rifles are operated by sliding the fore-end to the rear, which ejects the fired cartridge, then sliding it forward, which chambers a new round. Not as popular as autoloading rifles, pump rifles do have a strong following particularly in Pennsylvania, where hunting with an autoloading rifle is illegal.

LEVER ACTION The familiar cowboy gun of the American West, lever action rifles are worked by pulling down on a lever located at the trigger and then returning it to a locked position. These guns are experiencing a surge in popularity arising from new cartridge designs that allow for accurate ballistic-tip bullets to be used in the tubular magazines.

SEMIAUTOMATIC Using a small part of the gas created by the combustion of a cartridge's powder, semiautomatic rifles automatically eject and chamber cartridges with each pull of the trigger. Also called "autoloaders," they offer quick follow-up shots that don't require the shooter to manipulate a bolt or lever.

MODERN SPORTING RIFLE
Built in the style of the M-16, widely known from its use in the Vietnam War, the modern sporting rifle is essentially a semiautomatic firearm outfitted with an ergonomic stock and protruding magazine that has long defined military arms. Also called "AR-type" rifles (Armalite made the first models in the 1950s), these firearms are not fully automatic.

20 TURN A UTILITY TABLE INTO A BUTCHER SHOP

Butchering a deer can be a chore that will make a mess of your basement and send you limping up the steps with a backache. This DIY butchering table will make your meat cutting a more pleasant experience. It's cheap, easy to store and clean, large enough for two people to work at together, and raised to a spine-pleasing height. Before butchering, clean the table with a 50-50 mix of bleach and water. Rinse it with distilled water. —T.E.N

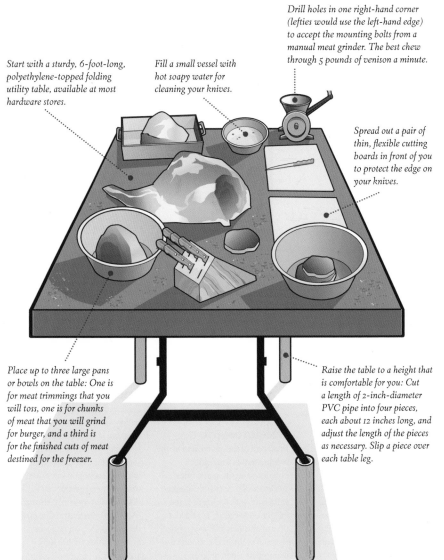

Drill holes in one right-hand corner (lefties would use the left-hand edge) to accept the mounting bolts from a manual meat grinder. The best chew through 5 pounds of venison a minute.

Start with a sturdy, 6-foot-long, polyethylene-topped folding utility table, available at most hardware stores.

Fill a small vessel with hot soapy water for cleaning your knives.

Spread out a pair of thin, flexible cutting boards in front of you to protect the edge on your knives.

Place up to three large pans or bowls on the table: One is for meat trimmings that you will toss, one is for chunks of meat that you will grind for burger, and a third is for the finished cuts of meat destined for the freezer.

Raise the table to a height that is comfortable for you: Cut a length of 2-inch-diameter PVC pipe into four pieces, each about 12 inches long, and adjust the length of the pieces as necessary. Slip a piece over each table leg.

21 HEART TO HEART

As we turn our backs to the glow of the truck's headlights, the still deer lies half-darkened underneath our shadows. Blood flecks its muzzle like beads of rain. Mud coats the hindquarters—it was no easy drag up the hill. The air is steeped with the earth-and-sweat musk of a buck in rut.

My 7-year-old son, Jack, holds one hind leg as I open the belly with a knife turned blade up. The skin tears open with the sound of a zipper. Jack's eyes are like moons. He talked nonstop during the long sit in the stand and during the hour after the gunshot and the dragging to the old barn. But he has not said a word since I handed him the hoof to hold. He has seen deer before: in the wild, hanging under the deck, on the butcher table in the basement, on his dinner plate. He has not seen deer like this.

I point out the liver, the bladder, the windpipe, the rope of intestines.

"Where's the heart?" Jack asks.

With one hand I part the red lungs, clasped together like a mussel shell. The bullet tunneled through the upper lobes, pulverizing the tissues that stain my hands and wrists. I remove the heart and wipe it clean of blood. It is dark and hard, unlike the other organs, which seem to quiver of their own accord.

"That's a heart?" he asks. I nod. He looks at it for a moment.

"Cut it open."

This is a startling request, and I hesitate, for it seems almost sacrilegious. But when a little boy is struck with wonder, there's no time to trifle, and I want this moment to go wherever my son wishes to take it. I cleave the heart with the knife, top to bottom, so the two halves sag open in my palm. The hollows of the interior chambers are dark. I squeeze the heart to show Jack how it works—how it pumps blood from the lungs through the heart and then out the arteries that branch, again and again, into the dendritic vessels that feed each cell of the body.

He is quiet at first, and I fear I've lost him. "Just like ours?" he asks, low and husky like he speaks sometimes. I hear in his voice the man he will become.

"Just like ours."

—*T. Edward Nickens*
Field & Stream, "My Boy Jack," *October 2006*

22 DISSECT THE WIND

Wind patterns are insanely complicated. One common mistake hunters make is misreading how currents react to landscape features. Missouri whitetail guide Kevin Small takes wind patterns apart with surgical precision.

It doesn't take a canyon wall to make the wind do flips. A hill, a ridge, a line of thick timber—all of these can have a dramatic effect on wind direction. Pick apart a buck's travel routes to find the one narrow window at which the wind is temporarily wrong for his nose but he has no other travel option. In this scenario, a west wind can work against you.

WIND WAVE When a breeze comes into contact with a large landscape obstruction, the wind will rise and then roll back over itself.

COULD BE TOO GOOD TO BE TRUE In theory, this is the perfect stand location (a) when dealing with a west wind. "But the wind will be rising at this point," Small says. "It will pick up your scent here and bring it right back to the bedding cover and the trails. You'll be busted 99 percent of the time."

SWEET SPOTS The only time to safely hunt these trails is in a north or south wind. In a north wind, hunt here (b). In a south wind, hang a stand here (c). —T.E.N.

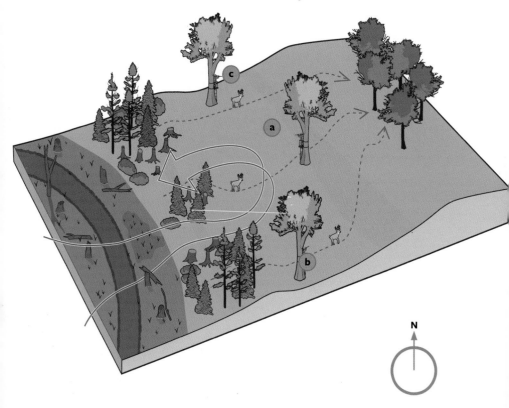

N

23 SEE IN THE DARK

If you've ever wished that you could see in the dark when out in the field, now you're in luck! With the simple steps detailed below you'll soon be able to maneuver just about anywhere in low-light conditions.

PROTECT In the critical minutes of dawn and dusk, shield your eyes from the sun. When moving your field of vision, allow your eyes to travel below the horizon line or shut your eyes as you move them. Before dawn, use the least amount of light required for the task; a low-level red or green light is best. Practice walking at night to increase your comfort level and clear favorite trails so you won't need a flashlight.

BOOST Use peripheral vision by focusing to the side of an object. Scan when you can; when your eyes linger on a particular object, they will adapt to whatever light is available. Try to get lower than the target to see its contours better. —T.E.N.

24 SHOOT YOUR OWN BIRD

Doubling up on one bird is the mark of the rank amateur—and a mistake even seasoned waterfowlers make too often. You and your partners need to discuss a strategy to avoid pulling the trigger on the same duck or goose. The gunner on the left might agree to take birds on the left of the flock or to shoot the trailing bird in a pair. Based on wind conditions and your decoy spread, figure out where the birds are most likely to fly and then hand out the shooting assignments accordingly.
—T.E.N.

25 STOP A RUNNING BUCK

A low grunt or bleat will stop a close-in deer most of the time, but you'll need to minimize your movements. Make a call holder by sewing a loop of elastic cord on one side of the upper chest part of your jacket. Slip a grunt call under the loop, and you can easily reach it with your mouth. If you can't risk even that movement, try making a squirrel-like tch, tch-tch with your mouth.

You'll want to have your gun or bow up and ready to shoot. Beyond 50 yards, a short, loud whistle sounds enough like a natural sound—a bird call, perhaps?— that it will hold your deer in place, intrigued but unalarmed, while they try to zero in on the source of this new sound. If you can't produce an ear-splitting whistle with your lips, buy a referee's whistle and slip it on your grunt-call lanyard. Caught without a whistle? Holler "Stop!" and hope for the best.
—T.E.N.

26 TAN A DEER HIDE

Tanning a deer hide with the hair on is work but it is manageable. Here's the drill.

Stretch the skin over a 2-foot-by-6-foot board. With a dull knife held at 90 degrees to the surface, scrape off all remaining muscle, sinew, and membrane. Rub copious amounts of noniodized salt into the flesh side, roll it up, toss it into a plastic bag, and freeze. Two to three days later, let the skin thaw, flesh it again, and wash out the salt.

Prepare a tanning solution of 4 gallons of water, 1 pound of granulated alum, and 1 pound of salt. Soak the hide in the solution for a week, stirring once a day.

Remove it from the tanning bath and squeeze it dry. Lather the flesh side with neat's-foot oil; let this soak in for a few hours. Stretch the wet hide over a hard, straight edge such as a sawhorse or table, and work it back and forth over the edge, as hard as you can, to soften it.

Use a rounded dowel or butter-knife handle for the hard-to-reach corners. If you think you're finished in less than eight hours, you're not. —T.E.N.

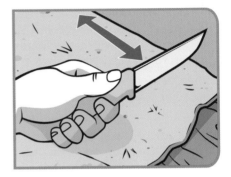

27 BE THE CAMP BIOLOGIST

Every deer camp should have a jaw puller to use to estimate the age of deer, if for no other reason than to have something else to talk about. Two tools are required: a pair of long-handled pruning shears and an inexpensive jaw extractor.

STEP 1 First, you'll need to lay the deer on its back; then, insert the jaw extractor between the incisors and premolars. Pry the mouth open.

STEP 2 Work the extractor along the lower jawbone, pushing down hard to separate cheek tissue from the jaw.

STEP 3 Use the pruning shears to cut the jaw as it curves upward behind the last molar. Place the cutting bar to the outside of the jaw and keep the handles parallel with the roof of the mouth.

STEP 4 Push the extractor through the cut. Put a foot on the deer's neck and then firmly pull the extractor out of its mouth. It will slide along the lower bone. At the front of the jaw, rotate the extractor 90 degrees to separate the jaws. Remove the freed jawbone. —T.E.N.

jaw extractor

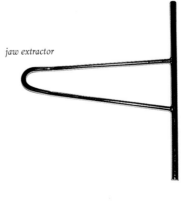

28 HELP A KID GUT HIS FIRST DEER

Now it gets tricky: You have a deer on the ground and a kid at your side with a face white as biscuit batter. Think carefully about how you introduce a young hunter to the labor of turning what was once a living, breathing animal into bundles of neatly labeled meat.

Don't make a fuss. Approach the animal as next year's supply for spaghetti and stew, and you'll send a subtle message: What happens after the shot is just another part of the process. Gutting and skinning is nothing to dread. It's as much a part of hunting as lacing up your boots, so treat it that way.

Don't push it, either. On the other hand, recognize that the notion of removing the organs and severing joints from an animal with a saw is not exactly a stroll through Candy Land. Go easy. You're not out to prove a point or toughen up a soft kid. Also, if you think you might have crippled an animal, get the child out of the picture immediately. Dealing with a wounded animal is difficult under the best conditions, and watching while you dispatch your quarry at close range might just be enough to send a kid into early retirement from hunting.

Be methodical. Talk through every step, pointing out the animal's body structures. And give the child a job. Even if she (or he) is too young to handle a knife, she can hold a leg while you open up the body cavity or pull back the rib cage as you remove the lungs and heart.

See it through. The learning experience shouldn't end with field dressing. Involve the child in butchering, freezing, and other preparation tasks. If a pile of bloody meat gives the kid pause, then assign another task. Ask for help running the vacuum sealer, turning the grinder handle, or loading the freezer. Help the child understand that a large part of killing an animal is devoted to sustaining another life—their own. —T.E.N.

29 LET A YOUNG DUCK HUNTER CALL DUCKS

Duck species that routinely whistle include bluewing and greenwing teal, pintail, wood ducks, and wigeon. Mallard drakes also make a sharp, single- or double-noted whistle, and, though the call is typically tied to breeding, it's a deadly finisher for shy greenheads during hunting season. For early-season teal hunting, a five-peep whistle is the go-to call. Since it's easy to learn, duck whistling is a great way to get a kid started. —T.E.N.

30 HOIST ANY LOAD WITH A BACKCOUNTRY BLOCK AND TACKLE

Maybe you're all alone and need to lift an elk quarter off the ground, hoist a food bag beyond the reach of bears, or hang a deer. Maybe you should know how to rig a backcountry block and tackle using nothing more than rope or parachute cord and a couple of lightweight rock-climbing carabiners.

STEP 1 This first thing you need to do is to find a tree with a strong, live branch that is at least 2 feet higher than you want to suspend the load. Throw a rope over the branch. Tie a loop in the rope about 5 feet from the standing end by making an overhand knot and pulling a short section of standing line through. Clip a carabiner to this loop.

STEP 2 Thread the running end of the rope through a second carabiner and then through the first.

STEP 3 Pull the end of the rope that goes over the branch until the first carabiner is near the branch. Tie this end of the rope to the tree trunk.

STEP 4 Clip the heavy object to the second carabiner. You may need to fasten a rope around the object.

STEP 5 Haul the load as high as required, using the tree as a block by passing the hauling end of the rope around the trunk. Pad it with a jacket or pack to lessen friction, and tie the hauling end of the rope around the tree.—T.E.N.

31 AGE DEER IN A BIG COOLER

Not all hunters have walk-in coolers, and a lot of us kill deer when it's still 70 degrees F outside. Here's a way to age whitetails for four to five days even when you're wearing shorts in the backyard. All you need is a whopping big cooler and a supply of 2-quart juice bottles or 1-gallon milk cartons washed out, filled with water, and frozen solid.

STEP 1 Decide whether to keep the hide on or off. Keeping the hide on prevents some moisture loss, but you'll have to contend with hair on the meat due to quartering the animal with the hide on.

STEP 2 Remove the tenderloins, which don't need aging. Saw off the front legs at the knees and then remove the legs at the shoulder joints. Remove both rear quarters in one piece by sawing through the backbone just ahead of the pelvis—you'll lose just a bit of backstrap. Remove the lower shanks. You're left with four pieces: the double hams, two front quarters, and the rib cage and backbone.

STEP 3 Place four to five 2-quart bottles or cartons of ice in the bottom of a large cooler; the absolute minimum size cooler you should use would be 160 quarts. You can use bags of crushed ice or small blocks of ice instead of cartons or bottles, but you'll need to monitor water levels carefully, and drain meltwater to keep it off the meat. Arrange the deer in the cooler—the double hams go in first and then the rib cage. Then, work the shoulders around them. Now tuck a few more cartons of ice in the space around the meat. Cover the cooler with a couple of blankets or sleeping bags for extra insulation. —T.E.N.

32 PICK THE RIGHT RIFLE CALIBER

Most opinions about cartridges are formed by a combination of shuck, jive, ad copy, and friends' ill-informed advice. On these pages you will find the truth, always unglamorous, sometimes downright ugly. And one of the ugliest facts is this: Choice of cartridge ranks fairly low in determining whether you will succeed as a hunter. If you're a good shot, it doesn't matter much what you use. On the other hand, choosing the wrong round can screw you up royally. With that contradiction firmly in mind, here are top choices in each category. —D.E.P.

SMALL GAME Light in the hands, easy on the wallet, these rimfire rounds are the perfect choice for hunting squirrels and rabbits. These are also used on short-range varmints.

1 .22 Long Rifle

2 .22 Winchester Magnum Rimfire

3 .17 Hornady Magnum Rimfire

VARMINTS Long-range, flat-shooting, hyper-accurate calibers with light recoil.

4 .223 Remington

5 .220 Swift

6 .22/250 Remington

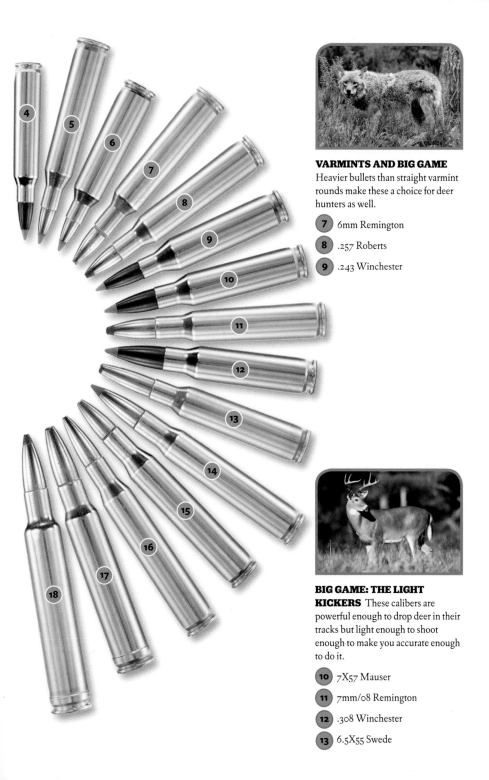

VARMINTS AND BIG GAME
Heavier bullets than straight varmint rounds make these a choice for deer hunters as well.

7 6mm Remington

8 .257 Roberts

9 .243 Winchester

BIG GAME: THE LIGHT KICKERS
These calibers are powerful enough to drop deer in their tracks but light enough to shoot enough to make you accurate enough to do it.

10 7X57 Mauser

11 7mm/08 Remington

12 .308 Winchester

13 6.5X55 Swede

BIG GAME: THE ALL-AROUND ROUNDS For everything in between antelope and moose, these calibers excel.

14 .30/06 Springfield

15 .270 Winchester

16 .280 Remington

17 .338 Winchester Magnum

BIG GAME AT LONG RANGE These calibers are ballistically capable of killing elk and bear some four football fields away. They demand similar capabilities from whoever pulls the trigger.

18 .300 Weatherby Magnum

19 .270 Winchester Short Magnum

20 7mm Weatherby Magnum

HEAVY OR DANGEROUS NORTH AMERICAN GAME These are large, tough calibers for large, tough game. Warning: They kick both ways.

21 .338 Winchester Magnum

22 .338 Remington Ultra Mag

23 .340 Weatherby

24 .325 Winchester Short Magnum

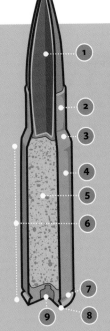

1. BULLET The construction of the projectile has a major influence on the success of the cartridge.

2. NECK Holds the bullet in place and aligns it with the rifling.

3. SHOULDER Modern cases have sharper shoulders–30 degrees or more–than older ones. It's thought that this gives a cleaner, more efficient burn to the powder.

4. CASE Always made of brass. There's nothing better.

5. POWDER It can be either spherical (ball) or extruded (log) and ranges in burning rate from fast to slow, depending on the bullet weight, case capacity, and case shape.

6. TAPER Modern cases have very little body taper; older ones have a lot. Low taper makes room for more powder, but cases with high body taper feed more reliably.

7. RIM Rimless cases have rims that barely extend beyond the extraction groove. Rimmed cases lack the groove and have wider rims.

8. BASE The base of the case carries the primer pocket and the headstamp, which designates caliber and make.

9. PRIMER Composed of a cup, anvil, and a small charge of explosive compound. Primers come in several sizes, and there are some with longer-sustaining flames, for magnum charges of slow powder.

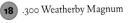

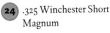
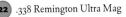

33 FILLET A DEER QUARTER

Boning out a deer quarter is quick and easy, resulting in tender cuts of meat void of bonemeal and marrow formed when cutting through bone with a saw.

STEP 1 Place the skinned hind leg of a deer on a sturdy table, with the outside of the leg facing up. Slice through the silverskin along the natural seam between the top round and the sirloin tip, and pull the muscle away from the bone. Cut the top round off at the back of the leg.

STEP 2 Remove the remaining silverskin. Cut the rump roast away from the top of the hip bone.

STEP 3 Turn the leg over. Using your fingers, separate the bottom round from the sirloin tip at the natural seam. Cut the bottom round from the bone. Then cut the sirloin tip from the bone. Slice the shank meat away from the bone and trim off connective tissue. —T.E.N.

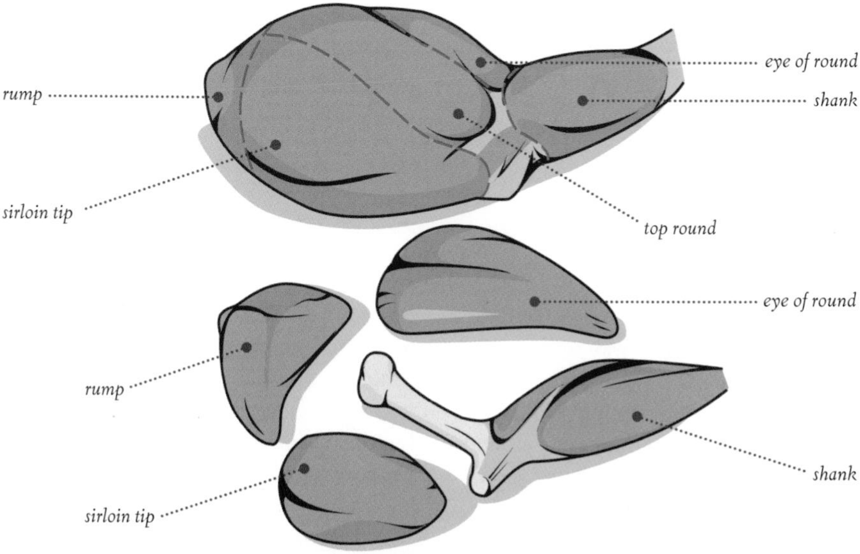

rump

eye of round

shank

sirloin tip

top round

rump

eye of round

sirloin tip

shank

34 SPATCHCOCK YOUR BIRD

You heard right. It's an Irish term that means to butterfly and nearly flatten a whole bird, so the meat cooks evenly. Use it to cook any gamebird over a fire.

Turn a dressed bird breast side down. With bird hunter's shears, cut cleanly up one side of the backbone and then the other, from neck to tail. Toss the backbone in the trash. Press the bird against a cutting board with the heel of your hand. Rub down with spices. Grill or spit it on a Y-shaped stick and roast it over the fire like a marshmallow. —T.E.N.

35 TAKE THE TENDERLOINS

These are the long fillets that run parallel to the deer's backbone inside the rib cage, under the saddle. They are the most tender cuts and deserve the most tender care. All that is required is a sharp knife to remove them, a quick rinse, and a trip into a plastic baggie fast to prevent drying. Besides that, they simply call to be sliced into medallions, pan-seared in real butter seasoned with black pepper and rosemary, and eaten with the fingers. —T.E.N.

36 DISAPPEAR FROM DUCKS

With so much pressure from eager hunters affecting these birds from north of the 49th parallel to the Gulf of Mexico, you'll find that head-to-toe camouflage is critical for all but the earliest flights of the season. In a salt marsh or over open water, a shiny human face peeking over the blind is visible to ducks from a half mile or more away. In timber, ducks are doubly wary, and anything that looks out of place will send puddlers into the stratosphere. Why didn't they commit after a couple of passes? Take a good look at yourself. Check your hands, face, and neck. Cover every inch, every time.
—T.E.N.

37 SIT AND HIT

Practice getting into a sitting position quickly so you're not floundering around when there's game in front of you. First, point your left shoulder toward the animal and sit down. Bend your knees so your legs flare out like wings. You're now quartered away from the target. Next, place each elbow inside a knee joint and find that place where the elbows just lock down. Now your body is a tripod: your butt and two elbows form a stable platform for your rifle. The trick is to do this often enough that you don't even have to think.

In a tree stand, you're already sitting, but you still have prep work to do. Keep the rifle out of your lap; instead, rest the fore-end on the shooting rail and the butt on your thigh. Practice aiming with the fore-end held in your hand and your hand resting on the shooting rail. Make sure you have a clear sight picture. If you're hunting over a shooting lane, you might not have time to adjust. —T.E.N.

38 REMEMBER FOUR KNIFE "NEVERS"

1 Never store a knife in a leather sheath. It can cause rusting or discoloration.

2 Never use water to clean a horn handle. Horn absorbs moisture and can splinter.

3 Never use hot water to clean a wood handle. If the wood is cracked or dried, rub it with olive oil.

4 Never touch the blade or metal parts after oiling. This can leave behind salt and acids, which can cause oxidation. —K.M.

39 ASSEMBLE A RIFLE REPAIR KIT

The most important 2 pounds you can carry on any (actually, every) hunt is a zippered nylon bag that measures 8-by-4-by-1 inches. It's a rifle repair kit, and it can save not only your bacon but the pork of other people who aren't so smart.

The cleaning rod is not for cleaning bores but for knocking stuck cases out of chambers. Any short and strong takedown rod will do. (A small-diameter rod works in all bore sizes.) Here are two other hints: Always carry a spare scope with a long tube that will fit a wide variety of mounts, and if you do work on a gun, do it over a bunk or a sleeping bag so when you drop small parts you can find them again. —D.E.P.

THE KIT SHOULD CONTAIN (a) a Lyman interchangeable-bit screwdriver, (b) a gunsmith bedding tool, (c) a Leupold multitool with Torx- and hex-head screwdrivers, (d) a set of small Allen wrenches (for working on triggers), (e) a collection of patches, and (f) a multisection .270-caliber steel cleaning rod.

40 KEEP FOG OFF YOUR SCOPE

Be careful as you bring your rifle up to aim that you don't exhale a cloud of moisture-laden breath onto the cold scope lenses. This will fog your scope in an instant. It's very easy to avoid making this basic mistake once you know what to do. Simply hold your breath as you bring the rifle up, aim, and shoot. Then exhale. —D.E.P.

41 RELIVE YOUR CHILDHOOD WITH A FROG GIG

For many rural kids, frog gigging is a rite of passage. For some, it's a summertime fling they never grow out of. Bullfrogs freeze in the glare of a bright light like the proverbial deer in the headlights. Remember to check local laws before you hoist your trident. Some states, such as California, prohibit the use of frog gigs but do allow enterprising herp hunters to hand-grab frogs, as well as bag them with nooses, hooks, and tongs (which would be something to see).

GEAR UP Bullfrogs are tougher than you'd think, so sharpen each gig point with sandpaper or an emery board. You can find gigs at sporting-goods stores and in mail-order sporting goods catalogs.

EYES AND EARS Listen for the deep gaa-RUUMPH of mature bullfrogs and then sweep a bright light across the shoreline of ponds, lakes, and riverbanks. Check out thick mats of lily pads, fallen logs, and low mudbanks. Twin pinpricks of eyeshine and the telltale crescent white chin give the frogs away. Let the little ones grow.

STALK You'll need to get close, so be stealthy. In a boat, it's a two-person job. The paddler should move slowly to avoid creating frog-spooking wakes and to keep the light shining directly on the frog. Stay clear of anything that will scrape noisily against the boat. You need to get the gig within about 6 inches of the frog before you make your move.

FROG KABOB Jab the gig hard. You have to pin the frog to the pond bottom, through muck and mud, so give it all you've got. Now, slide your hand down the gig handle to the spear points and grasp the frog firmly around the belly. Bring the frog and gig up together before removing the frog from the gig. If you're grabbing bare-handed, do it with gusto. Using a fish-cleaning glove can help you hang on. —T.E.N.

42 SKIN A DEER

The traditional skinning knife has an upswept blade and a high point, but a drop-point blade will do, if you take care not to puncture the skin with the tip. It's much easier to skin a deer when the skin is still warm. You can peel most of the hide away from the body by pulling on it, with your blade coming into play only to free the skin from the carcass at sticking points and for making initial cuts along the belly and chest, around the neck and hocks, and on the inside of the legs. Hold the blade so that the edge does not face your off hand, which grips the skin. Use shallow, careful slices to tease at the juncture of skin and carcass.

THE INITIAL CUTS

Make the cut along the inside leg with the blade facing up, so that it doesn't cut through hairs. If you do cut through the hairs, they can end up getting onto the meat, where they will be hard to remove.

FREEING UP STICKING POINTS

Most of your work will be done with just your hands. Use the knife sparingly to make small slices when the hide is sticking.

PEELING THE HIDE

Place a forefinger or thumb on top of your knife for precision while cutting. Peel the skin away from the meat with your noncutting hand.
—K.M.

43 SHARE THE BIRDS

You know it, and your buddies know it: One side of the blind is the King Daddy seat—the coveted downwind edge where the shooting is easy as the ducks drift in with wings spread a mile wide. Don't hog it. Seat placement can make the difference between fast shooting and hard feelings, especially when three or more gunners are in the blind. If there's an obvious hot spot in the blind, rotate the seating. —T.E.N.

44 SHOOT DOWNHILL AND UPHILL

Let's settle this old argument right here, and we won't need cosine angles. This is hunting, not geometry. Gravity only affects a bullet or arrow along its horizontal distance, not the linear distance taken by the projectile. To calculate your hold, simply figure out the distance between you and the target on a horizontal line. If you're 20 feet high in a tree and the deer is 3 yards from the base of the tree, then hold for 3 yards. If the ram is 200 feet above you, on a ledge 300 yards away on a horizontal line, hold for 300 yards and pull the trigger. —T.E.N.

45 KNOW WHEN TO SWITCH YOUR DECOY SETUP

Too many duck hunters toss out the decoys in the dark and then refuse to adjust the spread to changing weather conditions. Ducks must land into the wind. If the wind direction changes, so should your spread. Watch willing but skittish birds for hints that your decoys need fine-tuning: Ducks that constantly circle and circle, "wanting" in but never committing, or birds that consistently pitch into the dekes 10 yards out of range, could be telling you that your setup isn't in tune with wind conditions. —T.E.N.

46 BUILD A ROOFED MEAT POLE

Most meat poles get the game off the ground but they don't protect it from rain or snow. This gable-roofed version does, and with style. The overall dimensions of the structure can vary, depending on the size of your club (and the construction skills of your hunters).

STEP 1 Mark the ground for four corner posts and two ridge posts constructed of 5-by-5 treated timbers. Sink the posts into 30-inch holes and anchor them with cement.

STEP 2 Attach a 5-by-5 ridge joist on top of the center posts. Allow for an 18-inch overhang on each end.

STEP 3 Nail in 2-by-4 or 2-by-6 rafters, allowing for an 18-inch overhang. Nail in roof sheathing of plywood or 1-by-6 boards. Cover with shingles or roofing tin.

STEP 4 Hang a 3-inch-diameter galvanized steel pole from the two ridge posts, about a foot below the ridge joist. Affix large eye screws or eyebolts to the ridge pole at 3-foot intervals. Attach a block and tackle to these when you're raising the deer up. —T.E.N.

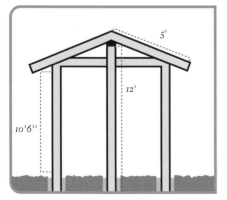

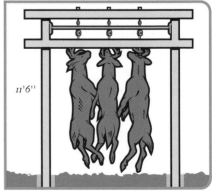

47 HOLD A SHOTGUN TENDERLY

Some shooters clutch their guns almost tightly enough to leave dents in the wood. Relax your grip, and you might start breaking more clay birds—or downing more birds with feathers. It's impossible to swing a shotgun smoothly if you strangle it. Try this: Put a death grip on an unloaded gun and mount it on an imaginary duck or dove. You'll feel the tension all the way up through your shoulders. Now hold the gun lightly in your hands and see how much more easily it flows to the target. How tightly should you hold a gun? Ever-quotable instructor Gil Ash says: "Just tight enough to squeeze a little toothpaste from a full tube." You may want to hold your gun even more lightly, tightening your grip only at the instant you make the shot so you can control the gun under recoil. —P.B.

48 KNOW YOUR FLYWAY

Pouring down from the northern United States, Canada, Alaska, and the Arctic, migrating waterfowl broadly follow one of four migratory routes as they flee winter weather for their warmer southern wintering grounds. Knowing the flyway in which your favorite hunting spot is located will help you track the weather patterns that drive ducks south. Watch for big storm fronts bearing down in the northern reaches of your flyway. Ducks will be on the move. You should be packing decoys. —T.E.N.

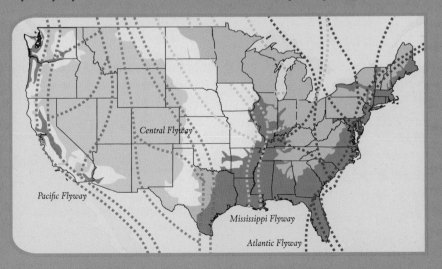

Central Flyway

Pacific Flyway

Mississippi Flyway

Atlantic Flyway

49 SOUND LIKE A DUCK

A happy-sounding quack from a 10-pound hen is the foundation of duck calling, but there's more to it than blowing hot air. Blowing a duck call well requires forcing air from your lungs by pushing with your diaphragm, and using an open-throated calling style to get enough air volume to shred cattails. Here's the practice drill.

STEP 1 Learn to blow from your belly. Hold a small mirror a few inches from your mouth and fog it with your breath, blowing deep, sharp exhalations. Even the quietest clucks and quacks come from that hot, deep, fog-the-mirror air.

STEP 2 To open your throat, sit down, tilt your head back, and look up. Practice blowing a sharp quack straight up at the ceiling. Master one clean, happy-as-a-clam hen quack. This is the most essential duck call, and you have to get it right.

STEP 3 Once your craned-neck, staring-at-the-ceiling quack is solid, slowly bring your head forward a few inches at a time. Master the single quack in each progressive position until your chin is level.

STEP 4 When you can maintain an open throat in a normal posture, follow the single quack with a second clean one, then a third. Tone comes next: Use quacks to work your way from the bottom of the scale to the top, and back down.

—T.E.N.

50 DECODE A DUCK QUACK

The best duck callers carry on a conversation with the birds they're hunting. Here's what they're saying.

HAIL CALL Loud and nearly obnoxious, used when ducks are too far away to hear anything but the most raucous racket.

GREETING CALL Warm and personal. "How ya doin'? What's going on tonight?"

COMEBACK CALL This is the waterfowl's red-hot party invitation. The gang's-all-here-and-you're-missing-it call to action.

FEEDING CALL When ducks hear this call, they should start thinking about a bunch of their buddies scraping their plates with forks. If ducks used forks.

HEN QUACK "Life is good, my friends. Grub a-plenty, and plenty to share."

—T.E.N.

51 BLAZE SECRET TRAILS TO YOUR STAND

Marking a trail to a favorite stand site or hidden blind is a dark art of the savvy hunter. Here's the secret formula.

CAMOUFLAGE THE TRAILHEAD Mark the entrance to the trail with a rock or other natural feature that is visible at night. Enter the trailhead from different angles to avoid wearing an obvious path in the ground.

BE TACK SHARP Flat thumbtacks reflect light at angles close to perpendicular, so they'll only show up if you're on the right trail. Cylindrical or cube-shaped tacks reflect light from all angles. Don't use them.

LEAVE CODED MESSAGES Use as few tacks as you can and devise a code only you and your hunting buddies can decipher. Three tacks in a triangle: Turn left. Single tack head high: Proceed straight. —T.E.N.

FIELD & STREAM CRAZY-GOOD GRUB

52 MAKE A TEAL POT

A duck dish made with pancake syrup and a can of cola? This is no joke.

INGREDIENTS
6 plucked and cleaned teal, or
   3 to 4 mallards
One 12-oz. can cola
3 medium onions, quartered
Smoked sausage, 4 to 5 links cut into
   3-inch lengths
Pancake syrup
Cajun spice blend

Place ducks breast side down in a large Dutch oven–style pot.

Pour the cola over the birds.

Add onions. Place one piece of smoked sausage inside each duck. Scatter the remaining sausage pieces in the pot.

Squirt each duck with a dollop of pancake syrup.

Shake Cajun spice blend over the whole batch.

Cover and bake in 300-degree F oven for 3 hours.

Serve with rice.

—T.E.N.

53 SET MONSTER GANG LINES FOR BIG WATER DIVERS

Diving duck hunters often have to contend with extreme decoy-setting conditions. This heavily weighted gang line will hold decoys in place through Armageddon but still give hunters the option of moving them when the birds need tweaking.

Tie a 5- to 10-pound anchor to each end of 150 feet of decoy cord. (A tip for hunters with retrievers: Use lead-core line to keep this long mother line underwater and out of your pooch's paws.) Tie in 18-inch dropper lines for each decoy, spaced about 6 feet apart. Tie in a metal trout stringer clip to the end of each dropper. Set a number of gang lines parallel to one another and fill in the gaps with individual decoys. —T.E.N.

54 BLEACH A DEER SKULL

Every buck is a trophy in some way. Make yours shine with this DIY bleaching process.

STEP 1 Trim away all flesh and skin and then boil the skull, removing it every 30 minutes to scrape away as much tissue as possible. Keep the antler bases out of the water, however; trim around them with a sharp knife. Use a straightened wire coat hanger to dislodge brain tissue.

STEP 2 Bleach will degrade the bone. Instead, use 40 percent peroxide, which you can purchase from a beauty supply store. To use, pour the peroxide into a spray bottle. Then on a sunny day, swab and spray the skull outside, being careful to keep the liquid off the antlers, or they will discolor. Repeat every 30 minutes or so until the bone is completely clean and white. This may take a few afternoons.

STEP 3 Glue any loose teeth in place. Use wood stain to restore faded antler color. Dry the skull and then spray the antlers with a clear semigloss polyurethane to protect them.

—T.E.N.

55 KNOW WHEN YOU'VE SCREWED A SCOPE HARD ENOUGH

One way that you can avoid endless trouble is by degreasing the base screws on your scope mounts and screwing them in hard. How hard is hard? Hard is when you're turning the screwdriver for all you're worth and the next thing you know you're lying on the floor and the dog is pawing at you and whining. Hard is when you're twisting away and everything turns purple and silver. You get the idea. When tightening scope ring screws, however, you do not crank on the screwdriver until all the little blood vessels in your nose burst. You crank until, with a reasonable amount of effort, the screws will turn no longer. Then you stop. That's hard enough. —D.E.P.

56 GLASS WITH A PLAN

Big, open country requires hunters to spend quality time behind good glass. Use spotting scopes and binoculars to visually pick the landscape apart to find that one memorable animal that offers a good chance for success. And you can't just lean over a spotting scope and rubber-neck distant ridges. Have a plan.

MAKE LIKE A PIRATE Spotting scopes can produce eyestrain-induced headaches. Consider wearing a patch over the eye you're not using.

BRACE YOURSELF You might be glassing for hours, so get comfortable and get rock solid. A backrest is key.

HAVE A FORMULA Be sure to avoid letting your eyes wander. Use binoculars first to pick apart the obvious cover. Then work a spotting scope over the rest of the landscape. Pick a viewing pattern and stick with it. Don't forget to look away from the glass every couple of minutes. Your trophy might have walked right up on you. —T.E.N.

57 CLEAN A SQUIRREL

Pound for pound (okay, ounce for ounce), squirrels are among the most difficult game animals to clean. Their skin is tougher than duct tape, and squirrel hair sticks to squirrel flesh with the tenacity of five-minute epoxy. Fortunately, you can create a simple device that makes stripping them a cinch. Here's how.

MAKE THE STRIPPER

STEP 1 First, draw two lines across a 5-by-3¾-inch piece of ¹⁄₁₆-inch aluminum plate, sectioning it into thirds.

STEP 2 Cut three slots from the long edge of an outer third (see below for slot sizes). Smooth the edges with sandpaper.

STEP 3 Drill two holes through the middle of the other outer third. Then bend the two outer thirds up at a 90-degree angle, so that they form a U-shaped channel.

STEP 4 Using the holes that you drilled, nail the squirrel skinner firmly to a tree or post at shoulder height.

SKIN THE SQUIRREL

STEP 1 Hook the squirrel's rear legs in the two narrow slots, its back facing you.

STEP 2 Bend the tail over the back and make a cut between the anus and the base of the tail, through the skin and tailbone. Extend this cut about an inch down the squirrel's back, filleting a ¹⁄₂-inch-wide strip of skin away from the muscle, but leaving it attached at the bottom.

STEP 3 Make two cuts, each starting at the opposite sides of the base of this strip and extending laterally halfway around the squirrel, stopping just in front of the hind legs.

STEP 4 Now grasp the tail and loosened hide and pull firmly down. Except for the skin covering the back legs and part of the belly, the hide should shuck off inside out.

STEP 5 Flip the squirrel around, and slide its neck and two front paws into the slots. Grasp the edges of the remaining hide and strip the "pants" off the squirrel.
—T.E.N.

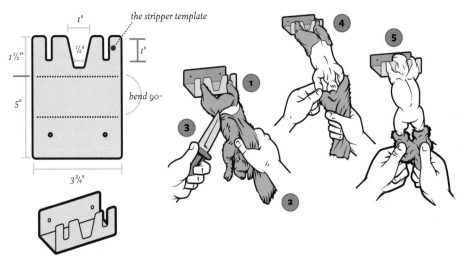

the stripper template

1"

1¹⁄₂"   ¹⁄₂"   1"

5"   bend 90°

3¾"

58 SCORE ON BIRDS AFTER THE FIRST FLUSH

Often duck and goose hunters will spend the afternoons walking up pheasants or bobwhite quail with their duck dogs or pointing breeds. Everybody shoots the rise and then whoops afterward. That's when a handful of late flushers goes up, and you're standing with an empty gun and your mouth wide open. You need to think a few steps ahead to maximize your chances.

STEP 1 Check the location of other hunters. Folks lose their focus after the flush. Make sure the group knows you're going in.

STEP 2 After the initial volley, take a few steps out front in order to get a better angle on late flushers.

STEP 3 Turn your stock shoulder slightly away from the location of the flush. This will open up your stance and give you a better swing on birds that flush in the opposite direction. —T.E.N.

59 MAKE YOUR OWN DEER DRAG

Prevent rope burn and your own heart attack by using a homemade deer drag. You'll need two black plastic pallet sheets in good condition (try getting them from a warehouse), a grommet tool, 20 feet of parachute cord, and 10 feet of drag rope.

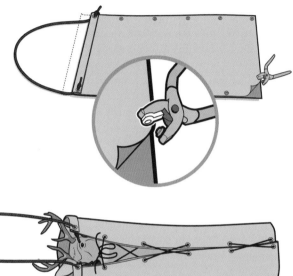

AT HOME Stack the two pallet sheets one on top of the other, slippery sides facing down. Attach them with grommets spaced about a foot apart all the way up both sides. Next, double over 2 inches of one of the short ends; secure with two grommets. Fasten the drag rope onto this reinforced edge with stopper knots.

IN THE FIELD Place your deer on the plastic sheeting. Use parachute cord to lace the plastic around the deer, just like lacing up a shoe. Get dragging. —T.E.N.

60 THREAD AN ARROW THROUGH COVER

The tight cover that is going to be holding those big whitetail bucks is also going to be tough on bowhunters. Say a good buck stops 40 yards from your stand, but there's a tree branch 20 yards in front of you—between your stand and the deer. Here's how to tell if you can make a clean and safe shot:

STEP 1 Put the 40-yard pin on the deer's vitals, as if you were taking the shot. Hold this point of aim.

STEP 2 Focus on the 20-yard pin. If the sight pin is above or below the branch, your arrow will clear. If the sight pin is on the branch, hold your fire. Your arrow's trajectory will carry it into the obstruction, leading to a spooked and educated deer or, worse, a wounded animal that will be difficult to track.

—T.E.N.

61 GREEN-SCORE A WHITETAIL RACK

To gain entry into the Boone and Crockett (B&C) record book, your deer must be measured by an official B&C scorer after a 60-day drying period. But you can get your own score by using any measuring tape. It's called green scoring, and here's the formula for a typical whitetail. (All measurements are to the nearest $\frac{1}{8}$ inch.)

Measure the length of the longer main beam. Then measure the inside spread of the main beams; if this is less than or equal to your previous notation, it's your first number to keep. But if it is greater, discard it and use the original figure instead. Call whichever you retain A.

For each antler, add up the following: length of main beam; length of each normal point (the beam tip counts as a point, but do not include its length in your measurements here); the circumference at the smallest place between the burr and the first point; and the circumferences at the smallest places between the first and second, second and third, and third and fourth points (or halfway between the third point and beam tip). Add the two antler totals together to get B. Take A plus B to get your gross subtotal, C.

Now for the deductions: Take the differences between the corresponding measurements of each antler—that is, beam and point lengths, and the various circumferences. For example, if the right beam is 2 inches longer than the left one, write down that amount. Do the same for each individual measure; total them. To this figure, add the lengths of all abnormal points—those tines that don't project from the top of the main beam, or that don't have a matching tine on the other antler. This is D. Subtract D from C for the score. —T.E.N.

62 MAKE YOUR OWN SCENT WIPES

Make your own scent-killing wipes and use them to wipe down everything from body parts to binoculars.

INGREDIENTS

2 cups 3 percent hydrogen peroxide
2 cups distilled water
$\frac{1}{4}$ cup baking soda
1 oz. unscented shampoo (larger chain drugstores will carry this item.)

In a large bowl, mix together the hydrogen peroxide, distilled water, baking soda, and unscented shampoo. Stir, pour into a one-gallon milk jug, and loosely cap the jug. Let the mixture sit for three days.

While that's marinating, fill a small, lidded tub about two-thirds full with plain brown multifold paper towels—the kind that come in stacks, not on a roll. Cover the paper towels with your homemade scent killer and mush it all around so the paper towels absorb the liquid. Squeeze out the excess scent killer and replace the lid. You're good to go—undetected. —T.E.N.

63 HANG A MOOSE (OR ELK, OR EVEN A SMALL HERD OF DEER) FROM SKINNY TREES

THE SUPPLIES

Carry a hatchet, plenty of parachute cord for making lashings, and five 30-foot lengths of ³/₈-inch (or thicker) rope. That's one rope for the cape and head, and one rope for each quarter.

THE INGREDIENTS

Cut three poles 18 feet long; each pole should be 5 to 6 inches in diameter. Limb each pole. Lay the poles on the ground in the shape of a goalpost. The horizontal spar should be about 6 inches below the top of the two uprights, which should be the same distance apart as the two standing trees. Lash the poles at each juncture using diagonal lashings.

THE HEAVY LIFTING

Now, the hard part: To raise the poles, place the top of the uprights against the base of the two standing trees, with a person at each tree. Lift the uprights and slide them against the standing trees—and catch your breath. A few feet at a time, raise the uprights to vertical. Lash the uprights to the standing tree as high as you can reach. Once the poles are in place, hang the meat. —T.E.N.

THE SETUP

Find two standing trees relatively free of large limbs up to 18 feet high, and no farther than 16 feet apart. Look for likely aspen in moose habitat. Lodgepole pines work well and are common in elk country.

64 FLAG A GOOSE FROM START TO FINISH

Flagging geese from layout blinds is the pinnacle of big-bird gunning. Here's an energetic three-step plan to plot the perfect deception.

FAR When birds are 500 yards to a mile out, get the whole gang involved. Everyone waves a flag as high as possible and then brings it down to the ground. Run around the decoys. Make a fuss.

NEAR The geese have turned and are boring in at 200 to 400 yards. All of the hunters should get in the blind.

The mission now: Look like landing geese. When the flock veers, reach up with the flags as high as you can, flag them six to eight times, then lower slowly to the ground. Do it again, but start lower. And do it again, starting nearly at ground level.

CLOSE When birds are inside 200 yards, the most experienced flagger should close the deal: Hold the flag at a 60-degree angle and then drop it horizontal. Bring it up to 45 degrees and drop it horizontal. Then start almost horizontally, and drop it to the ground, feather pattern up. You're trying to mimic geese on the ground stretching their wings. —T.E.N.

65 SILENCE YOUR TREE CLIMBER

ISOLATE THE PROBLEM At home, attach your stand to a tree a foot or two off the ground. Wear hunting clothes, grab your gun or bow, and climb on. Stretch your legs. Shoulder your gun and twist to each side. Draw your bow. Make a note of every place where metal or hard plastic comes into contact with the stand. Insulate the offending places with closed-cell foam or camouflage tape.

WALK SILENTLY Secure loose cables, buckles, and other noisemakers that could spook deer on your walk into the woods.

LUBRICATE MOVING PARTS Lube all squeaky hinges, welds, and joints with scent-free oil.

WAX SLIDING RAILS Run a scent-free candle across all rails that slide into larger-diameter tubes to dampen the sound of adjusting the stand.

LAY DOWN CARPET Glue a layer of marine carpet to the stand platform to silence scraping feet.

MINIMIZE ACCESSORIES The more gadgets you carry in your pockets, the likelier you'll sound like spare change clinking in the trees. Extra ammo, flashlights, and other small items should go into a daypack, to be fastened around the tree or hung from your stand. —T.E.N.

66 WALK LIKE A DEER

Moving whitetails generally stop on odd-numbered steps—three, five, seven, and so on. It's an irregular cadence that you should try to duplicate when tracking over crunchy snow, tricking deer into thinking that the intruder has four legs instead of two. —K.M.

67 MAKE BUTTONS AND ZIPPER PULLS FROM A DEER RACK

Racks that are too small to show off can still be put to use—they're sized perfectly for handmade buttons and zipper pulls.

To make a button, use a hacksaw to cut off a tine at the diameter you need.

STEP 1 Using the tag end of the tine as a handle, sand the cut surface. Use 80-grit sandpaper first and then 120-grit. Next, saw off a disk about $^3/_{16}$-inch thick and buff the other side.

STEP 2 Drill thread holes with a $^3/_{32}$-inch bit, spacing the holes evenly.

To make a zipper pull, saw off a tine about an inch long.

STEP 1 Smooth the surface with sandpaper and drill a small hole into the center of the antler, about $^1/_2$ inch deep. Fill this with a few drops of five-minute epoxy and thread a small screw eye into the hole.

STEP 2 Attach the pull to the zipper with a small loop of rawhide or ribbon. —T.E.N.

68 GRIND BURGER LIKE A PRO

The off taste in a bad venison burger often comes from fat, connective tissue, bone dust, and marrow. Want to get rid of it all? Be your own butcher.

TRIM LIKE A MADMAN Use cuts no lower than the shanks and trim as much of the fat, tendons, and connective tissue as possible. The thin, flexible blade of a pointed paring knife slides smoothly between connective tissue and flesh. Wash it frequently to keep it from sticking.

GRIND IT RIGHT Use the coarse blade for this. Electric grinders are easy to operate, but a high-quality hand cranker churns through 5 pounds of meat in a single minute and is a snap to clean.

HOLD THE FATS Despite all advice to the contrary, do not add extra fat at this stage. Instead, freeze packages of pure ground venison and mix it later, depending on the recipe, with binding agents such as ground chuck or pork, bread crumbs, or eggs. —T.E.N.

69 SHOOT STANDING WITH SHOOTING STICKS

STEP 1 Stand up straight. Adjust the height of the shooting sticks to adjust point of impact up or down. Never crouch or stand taller than whatever is comfortable.

STEP 2 Place the fore-end of the rifle in the V-notch of the sticks. Next, reach your fore-end hand across your body, under the gunstock, and into the opposite armpit. Gently clamp down on your hand to lock the arm in position. Now pull the stock into your shoulder, but not too tight. The goal is to be relaxed and put as little torque on the rifle as possible.

STEP 3 To fire, breathe deep and then let it out slowly. Squeeze the trigger just as you are running out of air. —T.E.N.

70 CHOOSE YOUR WEAPON FOR SQUIRRELS

Rimfire or scattergun? The decision is as much about philosophy as it is about ballistics. On the one hand, the squirrel is as sporting a .22 target as exists. On the other, they are tasty. Match the tool to the task.

USE A .22 RIFLE WHEN

• Hunting in a light rain. Stalking squirrels in the wet woods is a true joy.

• Hunting a dense population. Use .22 short ammo. It packs enough wallop out to 50 yards, but its softer report will keep squirrels active after a shot.

• Hunting fox squirrels. Slower and more prone to walk along the ground, these trophy-sized squirrels deserve a Boone and Crockett category of their own. Sniper them from 75 yards or better.

• There's a 48-hour *Rambo* marathon on television. Pack a semiauto and get it out of your system.

USE A SHOTGUN WHEN

• You hunt the early season. Leafy foliage makes rifle hunting exasperating.

• There's wind. Breeze-blown branches jack normally squirrelly squirrels into a level of physical schizophrenia unknown in the animal kingdom. Your only hope is a wide pattern.

• You want to walk. Follow creek banks and logging roads deep into the lair of the delicious tree rat. Shoot quickly and don't stop till something's falling.

• You're hungry. A hankering for squirrel is nature's way of telling you to forget sport and go big-bore. —T.E.N.

71 TUNE-UP YOUR TURKEY SKILLS

Often even the sweetest-sounding box calls come out of storage sounding a little flat. It's easy to ruin a call through overzealous tuning, so the secret is to go easy.

STEP 1 Cleaning comes first, but be very careful not to change the contours of the call's lips and paddle. Forgo the sandpaper. Instead try a light touch with a plastic-coated sponge of the kind usually used to scrub pots without scratching them. The plan is to remove hand grease, dirt, and old chalk, not wood.

STEP 2 Once the wood is cleaned, re-chalk the underside of the paddle. Many call-makers prefer to use railroad chalk, the type that is used to mark the sides of boxcars, but now there are many brands that are sold specifically for turkey calls. Stay away from blackboard chalk or any type of chalk made with oil.

STEP 3 Play the call, listening for the desired tone. Shiny spots on the lid's underside indicate that oil or dirt is still present. Repeat Step 1 until you get the sweet notes.

STEP 4 Adjust the tension screw on the paddle as a last resort. On most calls, it's right where it needs to be. Your goal is just to get the screw back into its original position if it has worked loose. Start by tightening it a quarter turn and then test the call. Repeat if necessary until you feel that you are tightening the screw past the point where it was set. If you reach this point, back off. —A.L.

72 TURN A FARM POND INTO A WATERFOWL MAGNET

The best farm ponds for duck hunting tend to be located near rivers and other large bodies of water or in flyways where ducks are known to move. Here's how to build a sweet farm pond duck blind—and manage the pond for a big return in feathers.

THE LOCATION Assuming a northwest to west predominant wind, place the blind along the southwest shore of the pond. Most dams are along the southern edge, and the deeper water will stay open longer during freezing temperatures. You'll never be looking directly at the rising or setting sun, and you can rotate decoys based on wind direction.

THE FRAME Build your blind in the spring so native vegetation can regrow. Forego tall blinds—make yours 4^1/$_2$ feet tall in the front and 5 feet in back. Top it with a half-roof over the back so you can shoot behind it. Add two 2-by-4s at an angle from the edge of the roof to the top of the blind's front to create designated shooting holes.

THE DISGUISE Start with a base layer of burlap, tack on chicken wire, and then use zip-ties to attach bundles of native vegetation. Pin oak, white pine, and cedar hold leaves and needles long after they are cut. Transplant willows by clipping saplings at a 45-degree angle and sticking them in the mud. They'll reroot easily.

THE LANDSCAPE Mow the north or northwest shore close to the ground and arrange five full-body sleeping-geese decoys. Geese like to loaf and sun in the open.

THE PLUMBING Draw water down a foot or two in early summer. Weeds and grasses will root on the shoreline mudflats. Reflood a few weeks before the season.
—T.E.N.

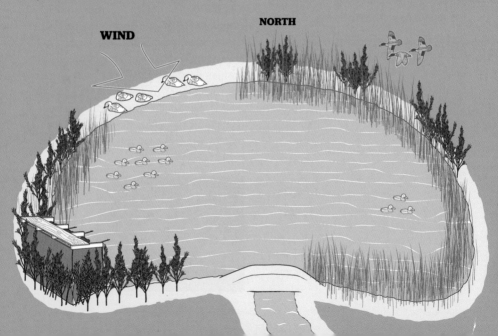

WIND

NORTH

73 SET UP FOR A DOVE SHOT

WATCH YOUR FEET Think about good shooting posture before your boots tangle in cornstalks and you empty the barrel behind a bird. A line drawn from your rear heel to your front foot should point to the place you expect to kill the dove.

GET IN THE SWING OF THINGS Resist the temptation to snug your gun to your shoulder when the birds are 75 yards distant. Instead, mount the gun as part of the same fluid motion you use to swing on the bird. You'll break your rhythm if the buttplate hits your shoulder too soon.

KEEP YOUR HEAD DOWN Watch incoming birds from the top portion of your peripheral vision. That way your head will already be lowered when it's time to put your cheek to the gunstock. —T.E.N.

FIELD & STREAM CRAZY-GOOD GRUB

74 MAKE DUCK, DUCK, JERK

Slowly drying rich duck-breast fillets turns out pungent, densely flavored jerky. Just about any duck will work, except for mergansers. Start with a basic soy-teriyaki mixture, and personalize it with apple juice, Worcestershire sauce, jalapeño peppers, brown sugar, and ginger. —T.E.N.

INGREDIENTS
4 ducks
2 tbsp. freshly ground peppercorns
1/2 tsp. onion powder
3/4 cup teriyaki sauce
3/4 cup soy sauce
2 tsp. rosemary
1 tsp. red pepper flakes
1 tbsp. liquid smoke
1 cup beef stock

Mix all marinade ingredients in a noncorrosive dish or plastic bag. Fillet the duck breast meat and then partially freeze or refreeze it; this makes the meat easy to slice. Carefully remove as much tendon and fat as possible. Slice 1/4-inch strips along the grain. Marinate them overnight. To prepare the jerky, use one of the following three methods.

(Regardless of which jerky prep method you choose, check the jerky often. Cooking times will vary widely depending on the type of cooking equipment, thickness of jerky strips, and how close the meat is to the heat source.)

• Smoker: Use the lowest heat setting possible for 3 to 7 hours.

• Dehydrator: Dehydrate for 8 to 10 hours.

• Oven: Spray the oven rack with cooking spray and line the bottom of the oven with aluminum foil. Drape the meat strips on the oven racks. Prop the oven door open 2 inches with a toothpick or short pencil. Cook at 150 to 170 degrees F for 2 to 5 hours.

When done, each strip should bend but not break. Store jerky in your refrigerator or freezer.

75 PUT A WILD TURKEY TO BED

Daybreak in the turkey woods is especially bright when you've roosted a turkey the night before. If you know where the bird went to bed, there's no need to blunder through the woods hooting. You can sneak right in and start your hunt in his bedroom. Here's a complete plan, from late afternoon through bagging a bird at fly down.

LATE AFTERNOON

LOOKING Turkeys repeatedly roost in the same areas. The places you've heard birds before make good starting points for an evening expedition. On unfamiliar ground, look for feathers and droppings beneath trees with large, spreading branches. Find a place where you can see and/or hear a long way (1). Don't blow your locator calls while the sun is up. Toms won't answer until they're safely in a tree.

DUSK

LISTENING At dusk, turkeys start flying up. Listen for wingbeats and turkeys crashing through branches, as well as for yelping hens and gobbling toms. If you don't hear anything, use a locator call. When you get an answer, slip closer (2), pausing to call occasionally until you determine exactly where the turkey is roosted. Stay out of sight and try not to get closer than 100 yards from the birds.

DARK

GETTING OUT AND COMING BACK
If you can see the bird, you're stuck. Wait until dark and tiptoe out. Mark the bird's location with surveyor's tape or punch it into your GPS. An hour before sunrise, set up 50 yards from the tree (3). Turkeys usually fly down to the uphill side, so cheat that way. Call softly and sparingly. If you got in undetected, the turkey will almost be in gun range as soon as his toes hit the ground. —P.B.

76 TIE A GETAWAY KNOT

Hunters on guided horsepack trips can help the wrangler out by knowing how to tie up their own mount. It doesn't sound like a very big deal until there's a game animal getting away and your guide has to deal with his horse, your horse, and whoever else's horse while you're all standing around. Learn a good hitch knot like the old getaway knot.

Start at chest level so the horse can't get a leg over the rope, and tie the horse with no more than 2 feet of rope slack between the halter and the tree.

STEP 1 Pass the rope around the tree on the right side (or over a rail).

STEP 2 As you bring the tag end of the rope around the tree, form a loop by passing the rope over itself. Lay the loop over the standing part of the rope.

STEP 3 Reach through the loop on the outside of the standing part and pull another loop of the working end through.

STEP 4 Snug the knot up to the tree.

STEP 5 To release the hitch, all you have to do is pull on the tag end and go. —T.E.N.

77 ENTICE A SHY BULL

When bull elk give Wyoming guide Terry Search the silent treatment, he turns to a cow estrus call. Here's his plan:

STEP 1 When bugles are few and far between, listen for the sound of a distant bugle, a closer grunt, or a bull horning a tree. Get downwind, settle into a spot, and make an estrus-cow call just loud enough to be heard.

STEP 2 No response? Wait at least 15 minutes. It's all about discipline now—do not call. Still no response? Make sure you can move without being seen by the elk and then relocate at least 30 yards away. You can move farther, but a 100-yard relocation, Search says, "would be pretty radical." Settle down and call again.

STEP 3 Play cat-and-mouse for two hours, calling and relocating every 15 to 30 minutes. If nothing happens in that time, back out carefully. The elk should remain close by as long as it has food, water, and shelter. Return later in the day or the next morning. —T.E.N.

78 STEADY YOUR RIFLE

After hoisting your gun with a parachute-cord pull rope, tie one end off around the tree or stand, and toss the line over a limb above your stand. In the loose end that dangles down, tie a loop using a tautline hitch. You can now move the height of this makeshift shooting rail by moving the knot up or down the rope. When it's time to take a shot, thread your rifle through this loop. —T.E.N.

79 ROAST A DEER HAUNCH

The 17th-century English poet and soldier of fortune Gervase Markham had this advice: "Stick it with cloves all over on the outside... larde it either with Mutton larde, or Porke larde, but Mutton is the best: then spit it and roast it by a good soking fire, then take Vinegar, bread crummes, and some of the gravy, which comes from the Venison, and boile them well in a dish: then season it with sugar, cinamon, ginger, and salt, and serve the Venison fourth upon the sauce when it is roasted enough."

Of course, Markham was writing in the England of 1615, when six servants were assigned to every respectable kitchen. Here's an easier way— if you're looking for an imaginative main course for your Christmas dinner, you can't do better than this. —T.E.N.

INGREDIENTS

1 haunch of deer
3 tbsp. ground cumin
3 tsp. garlic powder
Dried diced cherries
3 tbsp. brown sugar
2 tsp. ground red pepper
Toasted pecans
3 tsp. ground ginger
2 tsp. Chinese five-spice powder
(enough diced dried cherries and toasted pecans to fill the bone cavity; will vary) —T.E.N.

Cut the shank off the hind leg of a dressed deer and bone out the haunch. Stuff the bone cavity with a 50-50 mixture of diced dried cherries and toasted pecans. Tie haunch with kitchen twine. Roll it in a spice rub made of the cumin, brown sugar, ginger, garlic powder, red pepper, and Chinese five-spice powder. Roast the meat at 350 degrees F until a meat thermometer reads 140 degrees F (rare) to 160 degrees F (medium). Slice to serve. Slice and bask in your own glory.

80 SLIP INTO A STAND WITHOUT A SOUND

Bashing through the woods on your way to the stand is a great way to kill a spike buck. Here's the drill for getting in position without giving your position away—the first step toward hanging a rocking-chair rack on your wall.

CHOOSE YOUR PATH Before the season, clear trails to your stands by trimming away anything that might brush against your legs. Cut back old barbwire fences if they're no longer used, or mark fence crossings with a small piece of surveyor's tape.

WEAR GLOVES Some serious hunters pull on lightweight jersey gloves on top of rubber gloves. This keeps human scent off stand ladders and any vegetation you didn't clear away before the season.

PREP YOUR STAND Rings, buttons, and zippers can clink against metal ladder stands. Wear gloves here, too, and take your time climbing to avoid brushing against the rungs. Before you sit, scrape away loose bark from where your back will rest. Draw your bow or shoulder the gun, and swing at places a deer might appear. Snip away any branches that might snag and create movement. —T.E.N.

81 PULL OFF A BUNNY HUNT ON YOUR BUCK LEASE

You have a deer lease but no bunny dogs? Now that whitetail season is over, you may be sitting on a world-class rabbit hunt in the making. Post a message on your favorite online message board saying that you'll trade access to your whitetail heaven in return for a rabbit hunt. The setup: You bring a couple of buddies and let the hound handler do the same. It's a win-win for everyone (except for the rabbits). Use your deer sense to fine-tune the rabbit hunt.

DRAINAGE DITCH Dominant bucks use these dense corridors to move across an open landscape. Rabbits will use the subtle trails as an escape hatch or a place to wait out the heat. Toss the dogs in or thrash through on your own.

BLOWDOWNS These were prime bedding spots, and you stalked close, moving as slow as molasses. Now, forget stealth: Jump on the trunks, bang on the limbs—even if the dogs have passed by.

LOGGING ROAD This was a scrape-line mecca during deer season. Use dirt roads and ATV trails to get standers into position without much noise.

SWAMP Just like deer, rabbits take refuge in the most tangled messes on the property. Use your hound pack to dislodge them from their safe places.

INNER WOOD'S EDGE Bucks love to rub saplings along the edge of pine thickets and open hardwoods. It's a great spot for standers as rabbits dash out of the thick pines to pour on the speed.

GROWN-OVER CLEAR-CUT This is core bedding cover for whitetails, and bunnies use it for that and more. Work it over thoroughly, and not just with the dogs. Get in there and worm your way around too. —T.E.N.

82 REALLY, REALLY TICK OFF YOUR HUNTING PARTNER

A duck-hunting buddy finally caves in to your ceaseless whining and takes you to his new honey hole. It's on the back side of public land, so of course you cross your heart never to set a wader boot on the pond without him. And you don't—at least until you line up another hunt with someone else. There is nothing illegal about this, but it is patently immoral. Such disloyalty may (or may not) be forgiven. But it is never forgotten. —T.E.N.

83 MASTER THE RUT

This is it. Thirty days to give it your all. When does are ready to breed, bucks are ready to do whatever it takes to line up a hot date. When they drop their guard, be ready to drop the hammer.

Pre-Rut Bucks are getting antsy as their testosterone levels rise and the amount of available daylight plummets. Mature deer move out of their swamp and thicket hide-outs and nose around for does.

TACTIC–FIND A CORRIDOR Find a place where thick cover with food value, like greenbrier, edges into open woods near doe-feeding areas, such as crop fields or oak flats, and climb a tree. You might spot a buck doing a little pre-scouting on his own. Or put doe meat in the freezer before the rut kicks in.

Seek-and-Chase Does are coming into estrus right and left, and bucks are in pursuit. Deer will literally be running through the woods, all day long.

TACTIC–SIT TIGHT Does are like rabbits—they don't like to leave familiar habitat. If a buck chases a doe past you without giving you a shot, don't move.

They could make another swing by, or, better yet, a bigger buck might storm the scene, ready to brawl. Scent bombs and other estrus scents can improve your chances.

Breeding Deer seem to have evaporated from the woods, because bucks and does are pair bonding. They might spend 24 to 48 hours together and move very little.

TACTIC–GO MOBILE Glass the edges of bedding cover thoroughly, looking for coupled bucks and does. If you find antlers, plan a stalk. You might also troll for bucks in between hot does by setting up in a funnel and using an estrus-bleat call.

Post-Rut Most bucks—but not all—are worn out and holed up in dense cover, seeking a safe haven where they can rest and refuel for the coming winter.

TACTIC–GO DEEP AND NASTY Put up a stand that overlooks swamp edges, the backsides of clear cuts, or steep brushy gullies where bucks feel cloistered. And check out old scrape lines. Does that didn't breed initially are coming into a second heat, and a few bucks will be on the prowl for their last dance of the year. —T.E.N.

84 JERRY-RIG A MUZZLELOADER SHOOTING RAIL

Let's say that you need a shooting rail and nothing around seems like a good candidate. The fact is, you and your muzzleloader could be walking across the desert, and you'd still have a workable shooting rest. Remove the ramrod. Grasp one end in your left palm and hold it in place with your ring and pinky fingers. Hold the fore-end between your thumb and index and middle fingers. Brace the other end of the rod against your belt. —T.E.N.

85 TAKE A KILLER TROPHY SHOT

Tired of boring, dark, fuzzy photos of your best deer? Here's how to create a photograph every bit as memorable as the moment you fired.

STEP 1 Arrange the antlers in front of an uncluttered background. Situate the hunter to one side, holding the antlers with both hands. A big mistake is photographing a rack against the pattern of a camouflage shirt.

STEP 2 Stuff the deer's tongue inside the mouth or cut it off. Tuck the legs under the body. Cover wounds with your gun or bow. Wet the nose. Wipe away all blood. The final touch: Slip glass taxidermic eyes over the buck's eyeballs. They work like contacts and prevent those ugly glowing orbs. They're cheap and reusable.

STEP 3 Take some pictures with a flash, especially at midday. This will help light shadows, such as from a hat.

STEP 4 Try something different. Lie on the ground. Stage a photo of the hunter dragging the buck out. Experiment with unusual angles.
—T.E.N.

86 MAKE A BUCK SCRAPE

During the early phases of the rut, making a mock scrape is a great way to get the attention of the big bucks in your area.

WHERE Your ideal spot is a trail or edge near a doe feeding area, upwind of your stand site. Look for a place where a small branch or sapling extends over the trail at about head height.

HOW Don rubber boots and gloves. With a stick, hoe, or trowel, rake bare a 2-foot circle. Work a gel-based buck urine into the soil—the gel scents tend to last longer than the liquid scents—and drip a drop or two on an overhanging branch.
—T.E.N.

87 CLAIM THE SHOT ON A DOUBLE

STEP 1 Immediately upon pulling the trigger, feign in outright astonishment. Play up your acknowledged incompetence: "Holy cow! I can't believe I finally hit a going-away bird." Accompany your exclamation with a small fist pump.

STEP 2 Wheel around to face the dubious crowd. Shake your head and grin.

STEP 3 When you're met with the inevitable disdain, quickly give honor to others. "Did you shoot at that bird? I'm pretty sure I was right on that lower bird in the threesome. You, too?"

STEP 4 Cave in now and you lose. Offer an apology that puts the naysayers on the defense. "You can have that bird if it's really yours. I mean, if you're comfortable with that." —T.E.N.

88 DECIPHER FLIGHT PATTERNS

Keep an eye on wingtips—when the ducks stop flapping and sail for a second or two, they're looking for the source of the calling, which means you're doing something right. Don't stop now. If a duck's tail is lower than his head, he's cruising and looking, and you've got a good shot at finishing him. But if he levels up, your chances are getting worse. Back off the call. Pull that jerk cord. And call hard "on the corners" as the birds are starting to circle and all you see are tail feathers. —T.E.N.

89 MAP YOUR SPOT

Buy a U.S. Geological Survey (USGS) topographic map of your hunting camp. Or, better yet, print a topographic map or a satellite photograph from Internet sources.

STEP 1 Glue the map to a single sheet of foam-core board (a cardboard and Styrofoam laminate available at arts-and-crafts supply stores).

STEP 2 Mark the heads of pushpins with the initials of hunt club members.

STEP 3 Each hunter should mark his stand location with his pin upon arrival and remove it upon departure. —T.E.N.

90 SIGHT IN A SCOPE ON A BOLT ACTION RIFLE

A bore collimator makes easy work of a complicated situation. But it isn't a requirement for whipping a bolt action into hunting condition. Here's a three-step process to sighting in a scope.

STEP 1 Set up a target 25 yards from your shooting position, at roughly the same height as your barrel. Remove the bolt and place the rifle firmly on sandbags or bags of kitty litter. Sight through the barrel and center the target in the bore. Then, adjust the crosshairs as needed to center the target, being careful not to move the rifle. Replace the bolt and fire one shot. Your point of impact should be less than 6 inches from the bull's-eye.

STEP 2 Readjust the rifle so that the crosshairs are centered on the target. Look through the scope and adjust the crosshairs to line up with the shot fired in Step 1; again, do it without moving the rifle. Now fire another shot. The point of impact should be within an inch or two of the target center.

STEP 3 Move the target out to 100 yards. Shoot a three-shot group, disregarding obvious fliers. Start with the elevation adjustment and move the point of impact to the desired location. (For most popular deer-size loads, a point of impact 2½ to 3 inches high at 100 yards allows for little to no holdover at hunting ranges. Check a ballistics chart for details.) Fire another three-shot group. If elevation is correct, adjust the scope for windage. Let the rifle barrel cool between groups. —T.E.N.

91 SHOOT THE TRICKY OUT-OF-NOWHERE STEALTH BIRD

Ducks and doves have a nasty habit of acting like wild animals, such as appearing where you least expect them. That means overhead and coming straight from behind, presenting a very tough shot. Here's how to make it.

As you rise from your seat, point the muzzle at a spot halfway between the horizon and the bird (a) as it is flying away from you. Pull the gun swiftly up toward the bird. Keeping your head up and your eyes on the bird, bring the muzzle straight toward its beak. As the muzzle approaches the bird on the upswing, circle the muzzle around and behind the bird (b). As the barrel reaches the top of this circle, bury your cheek into the stock as you prepare to swing down and past the bird.

Pull down and through the bird, accelerating the swing as you blot out the target (c). You'll lose sight of it momentarily but fire as soon as you see a slice of sky between the bead and bird. —T.E.N.

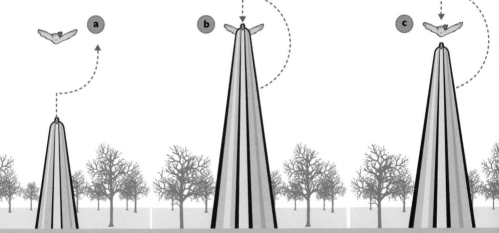

92 MAKE YOUR OWN COVER SCENT

To collect urine while field-dressing your buck, puncture the bladder and fill a small glass bottle with the stuff. Store it in the freezer. Cut off the tarsal glands and trim everything away, leaving only the dark, malodorous centers. Chop these into small pieces—hide and hair together—and pack it into the bottom of a small glass bottle. Cover it with propylene glycol and keep the resulting solution in a warm place—the top of a water heater is perfect. A day or two before you hit the woods, strain out the solids and mix in a dollop of thawed urine. Urine plus tarsal scent is as natural as it gets. —T.E.N.

93 PACK A WOODSTOVE FOR A SLOW, LONG BURN

You won't need to leave your cozy bunk in order to feed the stove if you load it right. Twenty minutes before sack time, rake all of the coals toward the stove's air inlets and stack large pieces of firewood tightly behind the coals. (Hardwood is best.)

Open the ducts wide for 10 to 30 minutes—a large stove will require a longer burn time. Once the wood closest to the coals has burned to a thick layer of charcoal, cut back the airflow as much as 25 percent. Starved of oxygen, the burn will slow down and work its way through the stack overnight.
—T.E.N.

94 CLEAN YOUR KNIFE

Fixed-blade knives need only a quick wipe down with a damp cloth after each use and a light application of honing oil on the blade.

Folders and multitools collect blood and dirt at pivot points and locking mechanisms.

If the tool has a plastic handle, immerse it in boiling water for one minute and then put it in a pot of warm water (so that quick cooling doesn't crack the handle). Scrub nooks and crannies with a toothbrush, working pivot points back and forth, and then air-dry the knife before oiling. Use compressed air to blast out gunk.

Wipe away surface rust with an oily cloth or 0000 steel wool. Carbon blades naturally discolor with use. Bring them back to near-original luster by rubbing them with a cork dipped in cold wood ashes. —K.M.

95 CUSTOMIZE BINOCULARS

Even the best (read "extravagantly expensive") binoculars on the market will give you a fuzzy view of the world until you correctly set the diopter ring. This adjustment, typically found on the right eyepiece or the center-focus knob, fine-tunes the binocular settings to compensate for any visual differences between your eyes. Set properly, a diopter will not only max out the performance of a high-end binoculars, but it will even boost the sharpness of budget glass. —T.E.N.

(a) Set focus for the left eye barrel.

Set diopter for the right eye. (b)

STEP 1 Start out by setting the diopter ring to the center of the adjustment scale. This setting is most likely marked with a zero; on some models it might be indicated with a hash mark or some other symbol. Cover the right lens barrel with a lens cap or duct tape.

STEP 2 Pick an object in the middle distance zone, about 50 yards away. Keeping both eyes open, move the focus ring (a) until the image is at its sharpest. Although you are focusing only with the left eye, keep both eyes open and relaxed. Do not squint.

STEP 3 Switch the lens cap or duct tape to the other lens barrel. Look at the same object and turn the diopter ring (see inset) to bring the object into sharp focus (b). Make sure the focus knob doesn't change. Keep both eyes open; do not squint.

STEP 4 Remove the lens cap or duct tape and look through both lens barrels. The image should remain sharp. Make a note of the diopter-ring setting, or place a small dot of fingernail polish on the correct adjustment. If your visual acuity changes during the year, you may need to reset the diopter.

96 PLOT A YEARLONG AMBUSH

You can carve out a cookie-cutter food plot, sure. Even toss some seed on an existing field and hope for the best. Or you can think critically about how to design a food plot that provides yearlong nutrition and season-long shooting opportunities. Start with a footprint shaped like a Y—the branched design allows deer to approach across a wide variety of wind conditions. Even if you can't build a better food plot from the ground up, these strategies can help you fine-tune any piece of deer ground.

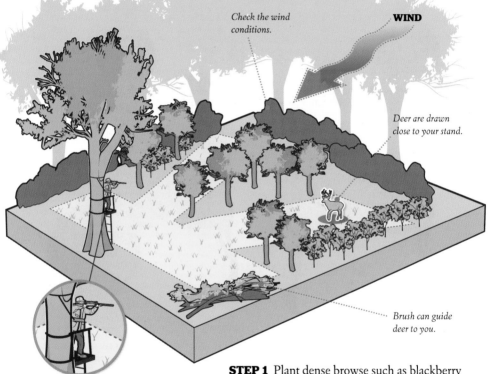

Check the wind conditions.

WIND

Deer are drawn close to your stand.

Brush can guide deer to you.

SHOOTING PLATFORM Camouflage your stand well, so you can avoid scaring off the deer that approach you.

KEY

dense browse

fruit and nut trees

STEP 1 Plant dense browse such as blackberry or the strawberry bush known as hearts-a-bursting at the upper, outside edges of forks.

STEP 2 Inside the Y, one fork should be planted in early-maturing greens for bow season. Plant the other fork in forage greens for late gun season.

STEP 3 Position the open end of the Y to face the prevailing winds in your hunting area and put your deer stand at the bottom end of the Y.
—T.E.N.

97 SOUND LIKE A DEER

Calling deer adds an exciting element to whitetail hunting. Here are the most important deer sounds for hunters. Each can be duplicated by commercial calls, and each requires practice to make it field-ready.

BUCK GRUNTS The deer grunt establishes dominance and signals aggression, often in the presence of a doe, so the right buck grunt at the right time can provoke a buck to move toward your position. Use a soft grunt to get a buck to move out of cover or take a few steps from behind a tree. "Tending grunts" are deeper and more urgent, often used when a buck is trailing a hot doe.

BLEATS Doe and fawn bleats can be ordinary contact calls or alarm signals, and deer will often investigate out of pure curiosity. A "doe estrous bleat" is a louder, drawn-out bleat made when a doe nears peak breeding time. A can-type estrous bleat call can be a deadly buck tactic during the rut.

DISTRESSED FAWN BLEATS Used to target does for the meat cooler, these high-pitched, urgent calls can also pull in curious bucks who want to see which does respond to an anxious fawn.

BUCK SNORT-WHEEZE This contact call is heard when two bucks rub shoulders over a food source or a hot doe. Use it during the rut's peak to troll for a mature buck or to pull in a buck that comes to a grunt call but hangs up out of range.

BUCK GROWL-ROAR Calls to replicate the growl-roar are among the newest whitetail tactics. As a buck trails a hot doe, its state of arousal climbs. Some bucks turn a tending grunt into a rapid-fire vocalization with a bawling, growling sound. Other bucks will investigate the scene of such intense activity. —T.E.N.

98 HUNT PHEASANTS LIKE A COMMANDO

Most pheasant hunts are group affairs, but the solo gunner shouldn't be intimidated by the size of a piece of pheasant land. Going it alone means you get to do it your way. And this is the right way.

HUNT STRUCTURE FIRST Key in on smaller habitat elements that will hold birds, such as tree belts, ditches, and thickets. Once you drive the birds from cover, you'll be more apt to put them up in a field. One great pheasant magnet to look for: the grown-up banks of dams. The thick vegetation provides a windbreak, food, and cover—and the confined spaces a solo hunter needs in order to succeed.

MOVE QUICKLY Speed up your pace and sprinkle in stops and starts. Nervous birds will take to wing.

WORK ROAD DITCHES In the late afternoon, birds move to roads to pick up grit. They won't want to leave their safety zone—until they see your boots.

LEARN FROM YOUR MISTAKES It's inevitable that you'll flush birds out of range. Take note of which side of the food strip they flush from and what routes they use to escape to cover. Learn how the birds use a piece of land, and you can fine-tune your drive next time. —T.E.N.

99 SKIN A DEER WITH A GOLF BALL

No hair gets on the meat, and this method stretches the deer out and lays it right down on clean plastic. It's like taking its pajamas off. Don't laugh, because it works.

STEP 1 Lay the deer belly-up on a sheet of plastic or plywood. Make an incision through the skin all the way around the deer's neck about 6 inches below the ears. Make another incision from the neck cut down to a point between the front legs. Continue this incision out the inside of each front leg as far down as you want to skin the carcass.

STEP 2 Working from the top of the deer, free about 6 inches of skin between the top of the shoulder blades, and insert a golf ball or golf ball-size rock under the skin.

STEP 3 Tie the deer's head off to a sturdy pole or nearby tree. Make a slipknot in one end of another rope and cinch it over the golf ball, making sure it holds the deer's hide firmly. Attach the other end of this rope to your vehicle's tow hook.

STEP 4 Now just strip the hide from the deer by easing the vehicle slowly away from the carcass. —T.E.N.

100 KNEEL FOR THE BULL OF YOUR LIFE

When you finally get a shot at the bull elk you've been working, it'll happen more quickly than you may imagine. It's vital that you practice shooting from realistic positions before the season. Here's how to make a shot from your knees, one of the most useful positions.

STEP 1 Start by dropping to both knees and lowering your butt to your heels. Some hunters prefer to drop to one knee only, but doing so can leave you susceptible to an unsteady side-to-side swaying movement, and this in turn can give you away or throw off your shot. The butt-to-heels drop creates a more compact and stable shooting position.

STEP 2 Keep the bow upright and rest the lower limb on one thigh (a). This leads to a lot less movement when you draw. If you were to lay the bow across the thighs, you'd have to move it upright to draw; at close range that's enough to spook a bull.

STEP 3 Depending on the length of your torso and the size of the bow, you may have to rise up off your heels as you draw (b). Doing this in one motion lessens the chance the bull will spot you—another reason to get used to this move in your backyard before your hunt.

STEP 4 To practice, staple 6-inch pie plates to your backstop. Move around, drop to your knees, and take the shot. Change angles. Go for accuracy first and then speed. —S.L.W.

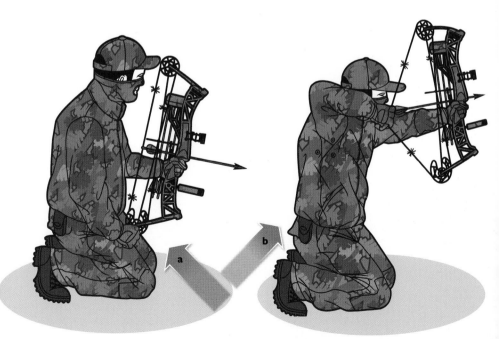

RESOURCES

(a) Thompson/Center Encore
Pro Hunter Turkey www.tcarms.com
(b) Perazzi M Series
www.perazzi.com
(c) Beretta Silver Hawk
www.berettausa.com

(d) Browning BPS
www.browning.com
(e) Winchester Super X3
www.winchesterguns.com

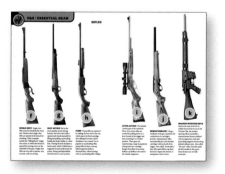

(f) Ruger No. 1
www.ruger.com
(g) Kimber 84M
www.kimberamerica.com
(h) Mossberg 500
www.mossberg.com

(i) Marlin 308XLR
www.marlinfirearms.com
(j) Remington 597LS HB
www.remington.com
(k) Stag 7 Hunter
www.stagarms.com

FIELD & STREAM

In every issue of *Field & Stream* you'll find a lot of stuff: beautiful photography and artwork, adventure stories, wild game recipes, humor, commentary, reviews, and more. That mix is what makes the magazine so great, what's helped it remain relevant since 1895. But at the heart of every issue are the skills. The tips that explain how to land a big trout, the tactics that help you shoot the deer of your life, the lessons that teach you how to survive a cold night outside—those are the stories that readers have come to expect from *Field & Stream*.

You'll find a ton of those skills in this book, but there's not a book big enough to hold them all in one volume. Besides, whether you're new to hunting and fishing or an old pro, there's always more to learn. You can continue to expect *Field & Stream* to teach you those essential skills in every issue. Plus, there's all that other stuff in the magazine, too, which is pretty great. To order a subscription, visit www.fieldandstream.com/subscription.

FIELDANDSTREAM.COM

When *Field & Stream* readers aren't hunting or fishing, they kill hours (and hours) on www.fieldandstream.com. And once you visit the site, you'll understand why. If you enjoy the skills in this book, there's plenty more online—both within our extensive archives of stories from the writers featured here, as well as our network of 50,000-plus experts who can answer all of your questions about the outdoors.

At Fieldandstream.com, you'll get to explore the world's largest online destination for hunters and anglers. Our blogs, written by the leading experts in the outdoors, cover every facet of hunting and fishing and provide constant content that instructs, enlightens, and always entertains. Our collection of adventure videos contains footage that's almost as thrilling to watch as it is to experience for real. And our photo galleries include the best wildlife and outdoor photography you'll find anywhere.

Perhaps best of all is the community you'll find at Fieldandstream.com. It's where you can argue with other readers about the best whitetail cartridge or the perfect venison chili recipe. It's where you can share photos of the fish you catch and the game you shoot. It's where you can enter contests to win guns, gear, and other great prizes. And it's a place where you can spend a lot of time. Which is OK. Just make sure to reserve some hours for the outdoors, too.

THE TOTAL OUTDOORSMAN CHALLENGE

If you enjoyed this book, we encourage you to check out the book it was excerpted from, *The Total Outdoorsman*. This collection of 374 skills covering Camping, Fishing, Hunting, and Survival will make you a true outdoors expert. You'll be ready to take on the world—or at least the wild. Go for it. But you might also consider displaying your newly acquired skills in another arena: the Total Outdoorsman Challenge.

Since 2004, *Field & Stream* has ventured on an annual countrywide search for the nation's best all-around outdoorsman—the person who's equally competent with a rifle, shotgun, bow, rod, and paddle, the person who can do it all. And whoever proves he can do it all walks away with the Total Outdoorsman title, as well as tens of thousands of dollars in cash and prizes.

The Total Outdoorsman Challenge is about more than hunting and fishing, though. The event celebrates our belief that the more outdoor skills you have, the more fun you can have in the woods and on the water. It celebrates the friendships that can only happen between sportsmen. Every year thousands of sportsmen compete in the Total Outdoorsman Challenge, and every year many of those competitors meet new hunting and fishing buddies.

So, if you're ready, you should consider testing your skills in the Total Outdoorsman Challenge. (Visit www.totaloutdoorsmanchallenge.com to learn more about the event.) And if you're not sure you're quite ready, you can always read the book again.

INDEX

CONTRIBUTORS

T. Edward Nickens (T.E.N.) is Editor-at-Large of *Field & Stream* magazine. Known for do-it-yourself wilderness adventures and profiles about people and places where hunting and fishing are the heart and soul of a community, he has chased ptarmigan and char north of the Arctic Circle, antelope in Wyoming, and striped marlin from a kayak in Baja California. He will not turn down any assignment that involves a paddle or a squirrel. Author of the magazine's "Total Outdoorsman" skills features, he also is host, writer, and co-producer for a number of *Field & Stream*'s television and Web shows, among them *The Total Outdoorsman Challenge* and *Heroes of Conservation*. Nickens has been a National Magazine Award finalist, and has won more than 30 writing awards, including three "Best of the Best" top honors awards from the Outdoor Writers Association of America. He lives in Raleigh, North Carolina, within striking distance of mountain trout, saltwater fly fishing, and a beloved 450-acre hunting lease that has been the cause of many a tardy slip for his two school-age children.

David E. Petzal (D.E.P.), the Rifles Field Editor of *Field & Stream*, has been with the publication since 1972. A graduate of Colgate University, he served in the US Army from 1963 to 1969, and he began writing about rifles and rifle shooting in 1964, during his service. He is a Benefactor Member of the National Rifle Association and a Life Member of the Amateur Trapshooting Association. He has hunted all over the United States and Canada, as well as in Europe, Africa, and New Zealand. Petzal wrote *The .22 Rifle* and edited *The Encyclopedia of Sporting Firearms*. In 2002, he was awarded the Leupold Jack Slack Writer of the Year Award, and in 2005 he received the Zeiss Outdoor Writer of the Year Award, making him the first person to win both.

Keith McCafferty (K.M.) writes the "Survival" and "Outdoor Skills" columns for *Field & Stream*, and contributes adventure narratives and how-to stories to the magazine and Fieldandstream.com. McCafferty has been nominated for many National Magazine Awards over the years, most recently for his February 2007 cover story, "Survivor." McCafferty's assignments for *Field & Stream* have taken him as far as the jungles of India and as close to home as his backyard. McCafferty lives in Bozeman, Montana, with his wife, Gail. McCafferty loves to fly fish for steelhead in British Columbia and climb the Rockies in pursuit of bull elk.

Phil Bourjaily (P.B.) sold his first outdoor story—on snipe hunting—to *Field & Stream* in 1985. Today, he is the magazine's Shotguns columnist and co-writer, with David Petzal, of "The Gun Nuts" blog on Fieldandstream.com. He is the author of the *Field & Stream Turkey Hunting Handbook* and, as a turkey hunter, has renounced early mornings in favor of sleeping in and killing spring gobblers between the hours of 9 AM and 2 PM. A 1981 graduate of the University of Virginia, he makes his home today, with his wife and two sons, in his birthplace of Iowa City, Iowa. He has traveled widely in pursuit of upland birds, waterfowl, and turkeys, but his favorite hunts are for pheasants close to home with his German shorthaired pointer, Jed.

Additional contributors: Bill Heavey, Anthony Licata, and Slaton L. White.

CREDITS

Cover images Front: Alexander Ivanor (bullet) Shutterstock (background texture) Back: Left and Center Jameson Simpson Right, Dan Marsiglio

Photography courtesy of Shutterstock, with the following exceptions: *Rick Adair:* 58 *Denver Bryan:* 28 *Bill Buckley:* 64, 71 (turkey) *Cliff Gardiner and John Keller:* 39, 95 *Google Earth:* 7 *iStockphoto:* 5, 41, 68, 72, 87 *Alexander Ivanov:* 3 *Donald M. Jones:* 60, 77 *Spencer Jones:* 32 *Rich Kirchner:* 31 *Holly Lindem:* 81 *Bill Lindner:* 133 *Minden Pictures/Chris Carey:* 73 *Neal and M.J. Mishler:* 221 *Jack Nickens:* 89 *T. Edward*

Nickens: 4, 52, 53, 93 *Dan Saelinger:* introduction (backpack), 19, 54, 71 *Greg Sweeney:* 45

Illustrations courtesy of *Conor Buckley:* 15, 32 *flying-chilli.com:* 73 *Hayden Foell:* 48 *Alan Kikuchi:* hunting icon *Raymond Larette:* 46, 47, 57, 91, 99 *Daniel Marsiglio:* 8, 10, 16, 22, 30 *Samuel A. Minick:* 100 *Jameson Simpson:* 2 *Mike Sudal:* 20, 37 *Bryon Thompson:* 98, 113, 133, 205, 260, 277, 282, 323, 362 *Lauren Towner:* 26, 33, 35, 67, 76, 92

Weldon Owen would like to thank Harry Bates, Kagan McLeod, and Steve Sanford for work done to accompany the original magazine articles.

ACKNOWLEDGMENTS

From the Author, T. Edward Nickens
I would like to thank all of the talented people who made this book possible, including the *Field & Stream* staff editors who guided this project with great care and insight. *Field & Stream* field editors Phil Bourjaily, Keith McCafferty, John Merwin, and David E. Petzal, and editor-at-large Kirk Deeter, provided unmatched expertise. Just good enough is never good enough for them. I wish I could name all the guides, outfitters, and hunting, fishing, and camping companions I've enjoyed over the years. Every trip has been a graduate course in outdoor skills, and much of the knowledge within the covers of this book I've learned at the feet of others. And last, thanks to my longtime field partner, Scott Wood, who has pulled me out of many a bad spot, and whose skillful, detailed approach to hunting and fishing is an inspiration.

From *Field & Stream*'s Editor, Anthony Licata
I would like to thank Weldon Owen publisher Roger Shaw, executive editor Mariah Bear, and art director Iain Morris, who have put together a book filled with skills that have stood the test of time—in a package that should do the same. I'd also like to thank Eric Zinczenko, *Field & Stream* VP and Group Publisher, for championing the Total Outdoorsman concept in all its forms. This great collection of skills would not have been possible without the hard work of the entire *Field & Stream* team, and I'd particularly like to thank Art Director Sean Johnston, Photo Editor Amy Berkley, former Art Director Neil Jamieson, Executive Editor Mike Toth, Managing Editor Jean McKenna, Deputy Editor Jay Cassell, Senior Editor Colin Kearn, and Associate Editor Joe Cermele. I'd also like to thank Sid Evans for his role in creating the Total Outdoorsmen concept. Finally, I'd like to thank my father, Joseph Licata, who first brought me into the fields and streams and showed me what being a total outdoorsman really meant.

Please visit our website, **www.garethstevens.com**. For a free color catalog of all our high-quality books, call toll free 1-800-542-2595 or fax 1-877-542-2596.

Library of Congress Cataloging-in-Publication Data
Nickens, T Edward.
Field & stream's guide to hunting / by T. Edward Nickens.
p. cm. — (Field & stream's guide to the outdoors)
Includes index.
ISBN 978-1-4824-2302-0 (library binding)
1. Hunting — Juvenile literature. I. Nickens, T Edward. II. Title.
SK35.5 N53 2015
799.2 —d23

Published in 2015 by
Gareth Stevens Publishing
111 East 14th Street, Suite 349
New York, NY 10003

© 2015 Weldon Owen Publishing

President, CEO: Terry Newell
VP, Publisher: Roger Shaw
Executive Editor: Mariah Bear
Creative Director: Kelly Booth
Art Director: William van Roden

Designer: Meghan Hildebrand
Cover Design: William Mack
Illustration Coordinator: Conor Buckley
Production Director: Chris Hemesath
Production Manager: Michelle Duggan

CPSIA compliance information: Batch CW15GS: For further information
contact Gareth Stevens, New York, New York at 1-800-542-2595.